Understanding Black Identity Extremism

Understanding Black Identity Extremism

Considerations for Law Enforcement

By Kyle Shideler

CENTER
FOR SECURITY POLICY

This book may be reproduced, distributed and transmitted for personal and non-commercial use. Contact the Center for Security Policy for bulk order information.

For more information about this book, visit **SecureFreedom.org**

Understanding Black Identity Extremism: Considerations for Law Enforcement is published in the United States by the Center for Security Policy Press, a division of the Center for Security Policy.

ISBN: 9798863194301

The Center for Security Policy
Washington, D.C.
Phone: 202-835-9077
Email: info@SecureFreedom.org
For more information, visit SecureFreedom.org

Interior design by ENC Graphic Services
Cover art by Matthew Franklin

Date: October 10, 2023

Contents

Introduction 1
Section One: Black Identity Groups 6

Chapter One
    Moorish Science Temple 8
    Formation and Ideology 8
    Moorish Science and Law Enforcement 12
        Moorish Science and Sovereign Citizens 13
        Moorish Science and Threats to Law Enforcement 16
        Moorish Science and Organized Crime 16
        Moorish Science Temple of America 18

Chapter Two
    Nation of Islam 20
    Formation and Ideology 20
        Malcolm and the Nation 25
        After Malcolm 30
    Nation of Islam and Law Enforcement 32
    Fruit of Islam 32
    Nation of Islam and Violence Against Police 37
    Nation of Islam and State Sponsors of Terrorism 42
    Section Two: Black Separatism, Marxism, and Black Liberation 47

Chapter Three
    Black Panthers 55
        Formation and Ideology 55
        Robert F. Williams and the Revolutionary Action Movement (RAM) 56

    Guns and Butter: The Black Panther Program 61
    Newton Reasserts Control 66

Chapter Four
    Black Liberation Army. 70
        Formation and Ideology 71
        BLA and Carlos Marighela. 75
        Assata: "Unreconstructed Insurrectionist". 77
        Black Liberation Army 79

Chapter Five:
    Interactions with Law Enforcement. 80
        Targeting of Police Officers: Traffic Stops. 84
        Targeting of Police Officers: Ambushes. 88
        Bombings and Hijackings 96

Chapter Six:
    Black Lives Matter and Other Modern Marxist
    BIE Incarnations 103
        Trained Marxists 106
        Revolutionary Grift?. 111
        BLM and Law Enforcement 114
        "Defund the Police" versus Abolition. 114
        BLM and Rioting 118

Conclusion 120
Endnotes. 124
Index. 158

Understanding Black Identity Extremism

INTRODUCTION

The Federal Bureau of Investigation (FBI) published an unclassified but sensitive document in 2017 identifying what it called "black identity extremists" that it considered "likely motivated to target law enforcement officers." The executive summary read:

> The FBI assesses it is very likely Black Identity Extremist (BIE) perceptions of police brutality against African Americans spurred an increase in premeditated, retaliatory lethal violence against law enforcement and will very likely serve as justification for such violence. The FBI assesses it is very likely this increase began following the 9 August 2014 shooting of Michael Brown in Ferguson, Missouri, and the subsequent Grand Jury November 2014 declination to indict the police officers involved. The FBI assesses it is very likely incidents of alleged police abuse against African Americans since then have continued to feed the resurgence in ideologically motivated, violent criminal activity within the BIE movement. The FBI assesses it is very likely some BIEs are influenced by a mix of anti-authoritarian, Moorish Sovereign Citizen ideology, and BIE ideology. The FBI has high confidence in these assessments, based on a history of violent incidents attributed to individuals who acted on behalf of their ideological beliefs, documented in FBI investigations and other law enforcement and open source reporting. The FBI makes this judgment with the key assumption the recent incidents are ideologically motivated.[1]

"Black Identity Extremist" is an FBI-designated category of:

> Individuals who seek, wholly or in part, through unlawful acts of force or violence, in response to perceived racism and injustice in American society and some do so in furtherance of establishing a separate black homeland or autonomous black social institutions, communities, or governing organizations within the United States. This desire for physical or psychological separation is typically based on either a religious or political belief system, which is sometimes formed around or includes a belief in racial superiority or supremacy. The mere advocacy of political or social positions, political activism, use of strong rhetoric, or generalized philosophic embrace of violent tactics may not constitute extremism and may be constitutionally protected.[2]

The FBI assessment proceeded to catalogue a series of incidents since the 2014 Ferguson riots involving premeditated attacks against law enforcement officers and evidence that those attacks were ideologically motivated. These included:

- The December 2016 attack by a former affiliate of the Huey P. Newton Gun Club, Micah Johnson, who killed five Dallas Police officers;[3]
- The October 2014 attack against three police officers by New Black Panther Party supporter Zale Thompson;[4] and
- The July 2016 ambush attack by Gavin Eugene Long, identified as a member of the black separatist "Moorish Nation" who killed three police officers.[5]

The assessment also cited several other recent law enforcement intelligence materials that had used the BIE category. By October 2017, the assessment was leaked to *Foreign Policy*, which published

"The FBI's New U.S. Terrorist Threat: 'Black Identity Extremists.'" The article featured only sources that universally criticized the document. The FBI made no attempt to defend the legitimacy of the report.[6]

The campaign that followed was predictable and appeared coordinated with the leak. On October 13, 2017, the Congressional Black Caucus (CBC) wrote a letter to FBI Director Christopher Wray demanding a meeting to discuss the intelligence assessment. On October 18, 2017, the American Civil Liberties Union filed a Freedom of Information Act request to access files on individuals identified by the FBI as "black identity extremists."[7] In a congressional hearing in November, members of the CBC pressured Wray to disown the assessment. The drumbeat of stories criticizing the FBI over the use of the term continued throughout the remaining years of the Trump administration. As Heritage Foundation Senior Fellow Mike Gonzalez described the campaign:

> At first, Wray was resolute, telling the committee he "will not withdraw intelligence assessments based on public outcry." But at another committee hearing in June 2018 Wray started walking things back. He said that the "feedback" had "promoted us to go back and take a very hard look at how we are bucketing the different categories of domestic terrorism…. I think it's been a useful learning experience for us, and I expect we will see some changes in how we do things going forward." By the following year, the walk-back was complete. At a hearing of the Senate Judiciary Committee in July 2019, Wray said in answer to New Jersey Democratic Senator Cory Booker, also a Caucus member, "we don't use the term Black Identity Extremism any more."[8]

From the beginning of the media firestorm, little attention was paid to

whether the term *Black Identity Extremism* was appropriate or whether the assessment was a useful intelligence product for law enforcement officers. The efficacy of the product was especially relevant at a time when officers faced a growing wave of politically motivated ambush-style attacks. Such attacks had increased substantially, year over year, during the same period analyzed by the assessment.[9]
Instead, the term was subsumed into larger political debates.

The term *Black Identity Extremism* suffers in part because it has been crammed into a larger Countering Violent Extremism structure upon which the FBI has relied for years, which favors imposed categories rather than addressing the motivations of terrorists or other proponents of political violence within the ideological frameworks understood by their adherents.

As a result, the FBI includes entities such as "Moorish Sovereign Citizens" alongside what it awkwardly calls "anti-authoritarian" actors, by which it probably means individuals motivated by anarchist or Marxist-Leninist-inspired "black liberation" rhetoric. Other BIE adherents are categorized as "supremacists" or "separatists." Additionally, the phrase *extremism* is itself a poorly defined term that no federal, state, or local government has any statutory responsibility to address, in contrast to legally defined terms such as *terrorism*.

Despite these issues, for the sake of convenience we will continue to use the term *Black Identity Extremism*, or BIE, to refer to groups and individuals whose motivations correspond to the definition offered by the FBI assessment.

This work will seek to demonstrate that there are indeed common threads running through a variety of different groups and ideologies covered under the category of BIE. It will attempt, as much as possible, to understand these ideologies as they are understood by their adherents—not to label these ideologies as extremist but to impart insights that may be of value to law enforcement officers who are called upon to investigate potential criminal acts perpetrated by those actors who do adhere to these belief systems.

This work does not intend to imply that any individual adherent to these ideologies is necessarily violent or will necessarily engage in criminal acts. It is to help provide law enforcement officers with an understanding of these ideologies when confronted by believers who do engage in criminal acts.

We will attempt to use both a chronological and an ideological framework. In Section One, we will address ideologies focused on questions of black identity in the strictest sense. That is, ideologies shaped around beliefs regarding the national or historic origins of African Americans in the United States. These include, most importantly, the ideology of the Moorish Science Temple of America (MSTA), as formulated by its founder Timothy Drew in 1913, as well as the ideology of the Nation of Islam, founded by W. D. Fard in 1930. We will also look at some of the historical events within both ideologies that resulted in significant law enforcement interaction.

In Section Two, we will look at the impact of Soviet Bloc subversion on the formulation of what came to be called the "black liberation" movement—a term itself based in the language of Soviet propaganda—and the interplay with black identity groups. Soviet propaganda efforts to provoke black separatism in the United States began in the early 1920s and transitioned into the Soviet strategy of supporting "national liberation movements" globally—including in the United States—in the 1960s and 1970s. The most obvious example of the impact of this effort is the Black Panther Party and its numerous splinter groups, most importantly the Black Liberation Army (BLA), which assassinated police and committed armed robberies on behalf of their cause.

We will conclude by looking at the impact of these two separate strands on modern BIE groups, including those that make up the political movement operating under the name "Black Lives Matter."

SECTION ONE
BLACK IDENTITY GROUPS

The emergence of alternative identities among black Americans, which form the basis for what might be called black identity extremism, emerged from the "Great Migration" of America's black population from former slave-holding Southern states to the industrialized North, beginning at the late 19th and early 20th centuries, as described by Judith Weisenfeld in *New World A-Coming: Black Religion and Racial Identity during the Great Migration*. Former residents of a largely rural Southern landscape, these new internal migrants began to explore alternative racial and religious identities in cosmopolitan Northern cities with broad ethnic and religious diversity.[10] This new diversity included black immigrants from Caribbean countries (most notably Marcus Garvey, who became the leading figure of Pan-Africanism) and interactions with Islamic believers (most notably the proselyting efforts of Ahmadiyya Sheikh Ahmed Faisal).

This period was one of intense debate within the black community in America regarding the identity and the name best used to describe their community.[11] Between 1886 and 1930, the Black Hebrew Israelites, MSTA, and the Nation of Islam were formed.

What these groups have in common is a powerful communal narrative that posits its members as the descendants of great nations with important, often mystical heritage and connection to the American continent. Black Hebrew Israelites believe themselves descended from the 12 tribes of Israel as named in the Bible. Moorish Science adherents believe themselves to be "Moors" descended from a North African "Moorish" nation that predates the founding of the United States. The Nation of Islam, which may have spun off from the MSTA, postulates that blacks were the original human race and that whites were a "devilish" creation by a mad scientist known as Yacub. It believed that the time had now come for blacks to build up the black community, shake off oppression, and establish themselves in a homeland in the southern United States.[12]

Throughout their history, these groups suffered from misunderstanding and suspicion from authorities, conflict with other black identity groups, the conflation and co-option of the identity by criminal groups, and internal divisions and factional infighting. This infighting resulted in seemingly endless splinter groups, which in turn formed yet more varied identities for their adherents to adopt.

Chapter One
Moorish Science Temple

Among black identity groups, few are misunderstood and mislabeled more often than those under the title "Moorish Science." Adherents of Moorish Science have long escaped simple classification for law enforcement purposes. During World War II, FBI reports on the MSTA reflected concerns regarding the influence of Japanese intelligence attempting to exploit the MSTA's identification as "Asiatic" rather than "African" but seemed to conclude that they ultimately posed no serious threat.[13] During the Global War on Terrorism, adherents of Moorish Science were identified as "a black Islamist sect."[14]

More recently, FBI documents and nonprofits purporting to track "extremism," such as the Anti-Defamation League (ADL) and the Southern Poverty Law Center, have attempted to identify Moorish Science adherents with the predominantly white Sovereign Citizens' Movement. All these classifications attempt to force Moorish Science ideology into a category of present concern for authorities, sometimes for political purposes. None seeks to understand the ideology as a self-contained system of belief.

Formation and Ideology

MSTA was founded in 1913 by Timothy Drew, who took the name "Noble Drew Ali." Drew Ali forged together elements of Ahmadiyya Islam (a relatively small and nonorthodox Islamic sect), the practice of various "secret societies" such as Freemasonry and the Shriners, and elements of Pan-Africanism espoused by Marcus Garvey. Middle East scholar Daniel Pipes writes:

> From this unique mixture, Noble Drew Ali concocted the 64-page scripture of his religion, the Holy Koran of the Moorish Science Temple of America (Chicago, 1927), which despite its name has almost nothing to do with the normative Islamic Koran but is largely plagiarized from two texts, one occult Christian and the other Tibetan. Even more strangely, his Koran focuses not on the figure of Muhammad, but on Jesus.[15]

According to a history of Noble Drew Ali offered by a member of the MSTA, Drew Ali was a member of Masonic Temple 459,[16] reportedly the first Masonic lodge in America to include free blacks.[17] Drew Ali apparently adopted ceremonial dress, a variety of secret handshakes, call and response code phrases, and other trappings from masonic traditions.[18] In 1927 Ali developed the "Holy Koran of the Moorish Science Temple of America," or "Circle 7 Koran," a short manuscript plagiarized from two earlier documents: "The Aquarian Gospel of Jesus Christ," by spiritualist Levi Dowdling, and "The Infinite Wisdom,"[19] which purports to be a work of ancient Tibetan teachings and is commonly used by Rosicrucian secret societies.[20] An MSTA meeting typically begins with a reading of the Moorish American Prayer:[21]

> Allah, the father of the universe, the father of love, truth, peace, freedom and justice. Allah is my protector, my guide, and my salvation by night and by day, through his holy prophet Noble Drew Ali.[22]

Invocation of Allah as a father figure and the invocation of Noble Drew Ali, rather than the traditional Mohammed as his prophet, is heterodoxic to traditional Islamic interpretation and would be considered heretical by modern jihadist movements.

MSTA followers assert that each nation has been granted its own prophet, citing Quran verse 10:47 as evidence: *"And for every nation is a messenger. So when their messenger comes, it will be judged between them in justice, and they will not be wronged."*[23] According to the MSTA, that prophet was Noble Drew Ali for the United States. This question of nationhood or nationality is of principal concern for the MSTA, which rejects terms such as *African American* or *black* (and earlier terms such as *negro*), which imply sub-Saharan African origin. Instead, the MSTA adopts the term *Moors* or *Moorish Americans*, with a claim to be descended from the ancient biblical Moabites, whom Drew Ali believed resided in what is today modern Morocco in Saharan north Africa.

Islam (or Islamism, as it is styled by MSTA followers) serves to further differentiate them. Eddie Glaude Jr., in his work *African American Religion*, notes:

> Islam functions here as a placeholder for an imagined community predicated on black self-determination. In doing so, and in [Noble Drew] Ali's hands, Islam becomes inextricably linked to an imagined freedom that is not bound by U.S. borders and white supremacist practices.[24]

Despite variances such as these, some MSTA adherents do follow classic Islamic injunctions against consumption of pork products or alcohol.[25]

This differentiation of the Moors as a separate national entity was vital to the group's self-understanding. Ali spun myths interlacing the supposed history of the Moors with that of America's Founding Fathers, alternately claiming that Moorish nationality was either guaranteed by, or suppressed by, the likes of George Washington and other founders.[26]

As early as the 1920s, Noble Drew Ali began making and selling "Moorish American" identity cards. MSTA adherents then proudly presented these cards as evidence of their separate Moorish nationality, and police reported difficulty getting MSTA adherents to provide information or follow lawful orders.[27] This behavior became so widespread that in 1929 Ali reportedly instructed followers not to display their cards, as it was causing "confusion."[28]

As the MSTA grew under Ali's leadership, it reportedly reached over 30,000 practitioners in several cities, including New York and Philadelphia.[29] According to Thomas Peele in his 2012 book *Killing the Messenger*, Ali eventually sat atop a thriving enterprise known as the "Moorish Industrial Group," benefiting financially from his instruction to his followers to emphasize self-sufficiency. The MSTA established businesses, including a newspaper and magazine, and became a political force to be reckoned with on Chicago's South Side. Ali also allegedly extracted sexual benefits from his practitioners, including at least three teenage girls, one of whom he reportedly impregnated.[30]

In 1928, Sheikh Claude Greene, a chief lieutenant of Ali, was stabbed to death within a Moorish temple. At least one history by an MSTA member asserts that Ali either ordered Greene (also known as Greene-Bey) killed after Greene attempted a coup within the organization or was misunderstood by followers to be seeking Greene's death.[31] According to Peele, Greene was the MSTA's chief accountant, had become suspicious of Ali's profligate spending, and attempted to extort a higher salary in exchange for silence. When Ali refused, Greene made the MSTA's financial records public. Peele records:

> Three nights later, a trio of men found Greene-Bey at the temple around 8:00 p.m. Greene-Bey led them to a small second-floor office. He apparently knew the men as fellow Moors and accepted them as emissaries of Ali. Minutes later, a janitor heard two shots. As he went to investigate, the three men rushed past him and ran out the door. The janitor found Greene-bey's bloody body; in addition to the gunshots, he had been stabbed four times in the neck and torso. Police noted

that it appeared Green-Bey was on his knees when he was killed.[32]

Ali himself was arrested for the murder of Greene but was eventually released. Ali died a short while later, although his exact cause of death is not clear, with stories ranging from death by tuberculous to having been beaten to death by his own parishioners.[33]

Upon Ali's death the MSTA suffered a series of violent schisms, with multiple temple leaders, including most notably Ira Johnson-Bey and Charles Kirkman-Bey, who declared themselves the successors of the Prophet Drew Ali. As a result, several organizations follow the essential MSTA model, which proclaim themselves the true Moorish Science Temple of America.

Moorish Science and Law Enforcement

The history of Moorish interactions with police are replete with themes of confusion and conflict over abiding by legal judgments and lawful orders.

From its earliest beginnings the MSTA struggled with charges of violence and seditious intent, beginning with Ali's national ID cards and continuing after Ali's death. In February 1937, Kansas City police arrested Harrison Green-El for assault and displaying a pistol after he stabbed another black man outside a Moorish temple. As Fathie Ali Abdat notes in *The Sheiks of Sedition: Father Prophet Mohammed Bey, Mother Jesus Rosie Bey and Kansas City's Moors (1933-1945)*:

> Thus, Prophet Bey's demand that Green El be tried under religious laws of Allah revealed a vast chasm between the Moor's preferred religious justice mechanism and Kansas State Court's legal system. Further the verdict shocked Moorish devotees who "had been taught that their faith was beyond the reach

of the law.... [I]t was impossible for the long hands of the law to reach out and jail one of their flock."[34]

Moorish attitudes on American law vary from temple to temple and city to city, mimicking Ali's own vacillation from "flirtation with anti-American sedition" to "overt gestures of American fealty."[35] Prior to World War II some Moorish groups adopted subversive Japanese propaganda themes aimed at black Americans, which resulted in an FBI investigation with inconclusive results.[36]

FBI documents show that in the 1960s, some MSTA adherents rejected Selective Service registration by disputing the legal definitions of their nationality and race.[37] The FBI records also show that such acts did not take place across all Moorish American groups, many of whom did register.

Moorish Science and Sovereign Citizens

Despite this long history, the ADL incorrectly identifies the "Moorish Movement" as an "afro-centric offshoot of the sovereign citizen movement that emerged in the mid-1990s." The Southern Poverty Law Center also insists on wrongly classifying Moors as sovereign citizens. Sovereign citizens are individuals who believe that, through a variety of legal and definitional loopholes, one can become "sovereign" and as a result not liable for U.S. laws, taxes, and regulations.[38]

This categorization is misleading and rejected by leading Moorish groups. The Moorish Science Temple of America, Inc., (one of the many MSTA splinter groups) notes that it:

> "is a holy and divine national movement, to teach our people those things necessary to make our members better citizens, obedience to law, and not to cause any confusion or to overthrow the laws of the said government but to obey hereby. We teach our people

of their nationality and divine creed of Moorish Americans, and birthrights, to love instead of hate, and that we are part and partial of the said government and must live the life accordingly. The Moorish Science Temple of America, Inc does not teach nor indorse [sic] or support any "sovereign" theory, or groups. Please feel free to contact us for duly qualified and authorized Divine Ministers."[39]

It is false to describe adherents of Moorish ideology as "sovereign citizens" when the behavior used to make this categorization predates the Sovereign Citizens Movement by more than 50 years.

Moorish adherents do not claim individual personal sovereignty, as sovereign citizens do, but rather claim membership in an alternative nation that exists in parallel with, but outside the authority of, the American nation. As one Moorish website notes:

> No "one" individual can be a sovereign. You will see if you study, your God or higher power is your sovereign, which is then represented by the head of the Nation and Government. So anyone wishing to be an individual sovereign is in error of law and Divine law.[40]

While some individuals identifying as Moorish Americans exhibit superficially similar behaviors in common with "sovereign citizens," the ideological basis for the behavior is substantially different. These activities include refusing lawful orders and videotaping law enforcement,[41] producing their own identity cards and car registration forms, and insisting that these be considered valid and recognized.

Additionally, individuals claiming Moorish affiliation have created documents claiming to give them title to others' property.[42] The typical pattern is for a perpetrator to attempt to present Moorish identity or property documents to county clerks or other officials, alleging original ownership of a property that is temporarily unoccupied, and to subsequently move in and change locks or otherwise attempt to demonstrate ownership. When removed by police and charged, perpetrators typically claim that, because of their Moorish nationality, police lack jurisdiction. They often declare extraterritoriality by claiming that the occupied property represents Moorish consular property covered under diplomatic conventions. This consular argument holds no legal status, of course, as the U.S. government recognizes no "Moorish" nation.

While much of the media coverage of these incidents over the past decade describes the perpetrators in these fraud cases as "sovereign citizens," nearly all the cases this author could identify mentioning "sovereign citizens" in the press involved self-identified Moors (and in one case a self-identified Black Hebrew Israelite).[43]

The effort to count Moorish practitioners engaged in illegality as "sovereign citizens" and therefore label them a "right-wing" or (even more absurdly) "white supremacist" threat can be understood as part of the same political narrative that has negatively impacted federal counterterrorism efforts and pressured the FBI to eliminate its BIE category.

Ignoring the Moorish nationality angle can also result in miscalculations. For example, in December 2020, Portland, Oregon, police attempted to evict William Kinney, also known as William X. Nietzsche, a self-identified "Moorish citizen."[44] The routine eviction devolved into a multi-day stand-off between Portland police and local anarchists and armed Antifa members who rallied to Kinney's defense in what was termed a "eviction blockade" of "indigenous land."[45] The Kinney squat had previously served as a safe house and gathering point for numerous local radical collectives.[46] Kinney's rhetoric aligned with local Portland anarchist and Antifa members because he claimed to be "indigenous," not because of "sovereign citizen" ideology.

Moorish Science and Threats to Law Enforcement

While most legal issues related to Moorish perpetrators are fraud and property crimes, there are examples of significant threats to law enforcement. Interactions with law enforcement have in some cases turned violent or included premeditated attacks, including the 2016 ambush attack by Gavin Eugene Long, who shot six police officers, killing three.[47]

Long identified as being a member of the Washitaw Nation, a Moorish subgroup that believes Africans were the original settlers of the North American continent and that the Louisiana Purchase illegally violated their right to the land.[48] Long was reported to have been associated previously with the Nation of Islam. In a suicide note found after the attack, Long detailed what he viewed as persecution by police, in particular the NYPD, against "melanated people," a term Moors traditionally use in place of *black* or *African-American*.[49]

In July 2021, 11 members of the "Rise of the Moors" group engaged in standoff with Massachusetts police after a law enforcement officer noted the individuals were wearing body armor and carrying long guns and pistols on the side of the highway. Eleven people were arrested, including the group's leader Jamal Latimer (also known as Jamal Talib Abdullah Bey). The group, based in Rhode Island, claims to be exempt from U.S. law and that it represents the armed forces of a Moorish nation.[50]

Moorish Science and Organized Crime

A few notable Moorish interactions with law enforcement had more to do with organized crime than ideology.

In 1976, Chicago resident Jeff Fort (also known as Jeff Fort-El) was released from prison following a conviction for misusing federal funds after the alliance of street gangs he co-founded, the Black P Stone Nation, was given grants for job training and poverty programs. The Black P

Stones—which had already reached the level of a powerful organized crime syndicate with control over the drug trade, prostitution, and extortion rackets—also had ties to local radical politics. Upon release, Fort-El joined the MSTA and reestablished his gang as the El-Rukn tribe of the Moorish Science Temple.

In 1979, El-Fort and his disciples sued the prison system to have the MSTA recognized as a religion so that its adherents could practice their beliefs behind bars.[51] While some MSTA adherents claimed that Fort-El had misappropriated the MSTA name and was not a member, FBI archives show that the El Rukns did use MSTA religious trappings and traditions, including the Moorish American Prayer, the MSTA "divine constitution," and a sheet of call and response questions commonly referred to as 101s (because there are 101 questions), all of which are hallmarks of the MSTA.[52]

By 1986 however, the El Rukns eventually claimed status as orthodox Sunni Muslims and begin to adopt more traditional Islamic terminology, including renaming the group's headquarters from a "temple" to a mosque and changing El-Fort's criminal lieutenants from "generals" to "emirs."[53]

Throughout the early to mid-1980s, state and federal investigators indicted and convicted Fort-El and the El Rukns on drug trafficking, extortion, murder, and even terrorism after the group attempted to procure an anti-tank rocket from an undercover federal agent to conduct terrorism for hire on behalf of Libyan dictator Muammar Qaddafi.[54] At its heyday the El Rukns' criminal empire, forged together by El-Fort's charismatic personality and syncretic Moorish ideology, reached a supposed 8,000 members spread throughout the Midwest.[55] Police also broke up the Security Maintenance Services, an unlicensed security firm established by the El Rukns.[56]

Jeff Fort-El and the El Rukns were not the only MSTA-linked organization to engage in organized crime.

In 1977, Jerry Lewis (Lewis-El), an African American man in prison for drug convictions, converted to Moorish Science. Upon release he formed the group's St. Louis chapter. Investigators later suspected that

Lewis was leading a criminal conspiracy, earning millions of dollars through drug trafficking and murdering those who opposed him.[57]

More recently, in 2014 three MSTA-associated Detroit drug dealers—Carlos Powell, Eric Powell, and Ernest Proge—were convicted for running a multi-million-dollar drug ring. Police seized $21 million in cash and large quantities of heroin, cocaine, and marijuana.[58] Like the El Rukns, the Powell drug gang had ties to local politics, with former Democratic State Representative Kenneth Daniels arrested for assisting the gang in hiding its finances.[59]

MSTA adherents have also been linked to Islamic terrorist activity. Clement Hampton-El served as a critical member of the 1993 World Trade Center bombing plot in New York. Narseal Batiste was the ringleader of a group that attempted to bomb the Sears Tower in Chicago.[60] The attack was thwarted by an FBI sting operation using an agent infiltrating the group under the cover of being a member of Al Qaeda.[61]

MSTA supporters can be typically identified by the wearing of red fez hats (for males) or turbans (for females), displaying the Moroccan flag (red flag with green five-pointed star) frequently together with an American flag. MSTA supporters may display a red crescent-and-star device, possibly with a scimitar beneath it often from a chain or necklace. MSTA members frequently use the greeting "Islam" and identify each other as "Moor."[62] Members are encouraged to add to their names the suffix -El, -Bey, or -Ali, which are intended to represent ancient Moorish tribes. Other symbols may include a black and white image of a handshake (sometimes with the word *unity* below it), and image of an eye (with the word *Allah* below it) and a crescent and star (with the word *Salvation* beneath it.)

Moorish Science Temple of America

Founder: Noble Drew Ali
Established: 1927
Summary of Ideology: claim membership in an alternative nation that exists in parallel with, but outside the authority of, the American nation
Subgroups: multiple groups claiming title as Moorish Science Temple of America, Washitaw Nation, Rise of the Moors
Estimated Adherents: unknown, but more than 4,000
Distinguishing Practices: red fez hats for males or turbans for females; displaying the Moroccan flag; adding the suffix -El, -Bey or -Ali to their names

Chapter Two
Nation of Islam

Despite its relatively small number of total members—probably between 20,000 and 50,000 total—the Nation of Islam (NOI) has had an outsized impact on black identity in America. NOI's long history with famous figures such as Malcolm X and Muhammad Ali makes it a household name. Its close ties with several influential and largely mainstream political figures have muted otherwise well-deserved criticism for virulent and often violent anti-Semitic and anti-white racial hatred, black supremacist attitudes, and a rap sheet of criminal behavior and violence. Additionally, NOI, from the very beginning, had documented ties to the subversive campaigns of foreign nations, from Imperial Japan's Black Dragon Society to state sponsors of terrorism such as Iran, Libya, and Sudan.

NOI's homespun and seemingly bizarre theology, which involves a mad scientist named Yacub creating "white devils" in a lab, has often led observers to minimize it and treat it as unserious rather than understand it within context as an internally consistent belief system that appeals to a certain subset of alienated individuals looking for identity and meaning. History is replete with examples of law enforcement serially underestimating and disregarding NOI, often to its own peril and that of the larger citizenry.

Formation and Ideology

Much of early NOI history is suggestive of a shared history with the MSTA, including referring to its members as "Asiatic." Like the

MSTA, there were early and credible allegations of ties to Japanese intelligence's Black Dragon Society, which was founded to subvert black loyalty to the United States in the leadup to World War II.[63] NOI also adopted the MSTA style of rote indoctrination in the form of written questions and answers under the name "Actual Facts" and "Lost-Found Muslim Lessons."[64] But instead of a national and ethnic identity of "Moors," NOI offers followers a racialized religious identity. Adherents are understood as black and indigenous to the North American continent, or, as the language of NOI would say, "the Lost-Found" "Tribe of Shabazz" in the "wilderness of North America." The language of NOI blames Christianity as a false religion that deliberately divorced blacks from their original religious identity as Muslims to enable their enslavement by whites, even while NOI teachings are replete with citations to the Bible.

The exact origins of NOI are debated. What is generally agreed upon is that an individual identifying himself as W. D. Fard, who claimed to have come from "the holy city of Mecca," formed NOI in Detroit in 1930 while serving as an itinerant peddler. His followers came to regard him as "the supreme ruler of the universe" and God in human form.[65]

A 1917 draft card identifies Fard as having been born in Shinka, Afghanistan, in 1893 and includes the alternative name "Ford." Other documents linked to Ford claimed he was from New Zealand or Portland, Oregon. The FBI later claimed that Fard was really Wallace Dodd Ford, a former convicted heroin dealer and small-time crook.

One plausible version of the story suggests that Wallace Dodd Ford joined the MSTA under the name David Ford-El and founded NOI after having seen the financial success of the MSTA. Ford-El was reportedly defeated in the succession battles that followed the death of Noble Drew Ali and so chose to strike out on his own.[66]

Fard remained the leader of NOI for only a short time before his mysterious disappearance, which appears to have been related to legal troubles after an NOI adherent, Robert Harris, murdered another black man in an apparent NOI cult ritual.[67]

Fard was succeeded by his closest confidant and assistant, Elijah Poole, later known as Elijah Muhammad. Muhammad played the primary role in codifying the NOI's theology. Edward Curtis, in his chapter on NOI for *the Handbook of Islamic Sects and Movements*, notes that Elijah Muhammad emphasized a grounded and "scientific" conception, beginning with the NOI's origin story:

> Many members who converted to the NOI said and wrote that they found Islam to be a more rational and scientific religion than Christianity. Even if many of the theological claims of the NOI were no more based on modern science than those of many Christian groups, NOI members presented their religion as grounded in material reality.... NOI catechisms entitled "Actual Facts", the "Rules of Islam", and "Student Enrollment", memorized by both male and female followers, offered both astronomical fact and cosmological theory. For example, "Actual Facts" detailed the various distances between planets in the solar system and the Sun as well as the total square mileage of land on the Earth. In explaining the separation of the Moon from the Earth, this catechism credited a scientist with creating explosion sixty-six trillion years ago. Indeed, the belief that scientists' mastery of technology was behind most cosmological events was central to Elijah Muhammad's thought.[68]

While the MSTA offers its adherents what might be called a "separate but equal" claim to nationhood and national/ethnic identity, NOI offers a promise of racial supremacy grounded in "science," a sort of mirror image of the Darwinian or eugenic racism common at the time of NOI's founding. As the first question of NOI's "Student Enrollment" questionnaire explains, the "Asiatic black man" is the "original man," "father of civilization" and "God of the universe." All other racial categories are derivative of these original men, except for whites. Claude A. Clegg III explains:

> Perhaps the best known, and most controversial, element of the Muslims' message was their contention that whites were devils. Briefly stated, in the belief system of the Nation, whites were created six thousand years ago by Yacub, a black god-scientist who had mastered genetic engineering. This process, called grafting, started with genes taken from black people, which were manipulated in such a way as to create hews [sic] of brown, red, yellow, and finally white skin color. As predestined by prophecy, the white people would be void of any propensity toward justice or righteousness and inclined toward all things foul, evil, and unjust. Yacub had incorporated these traits into their nature. They would be given six thousand years to rule, plus a grace period, all of which would end in the late twentieth century.[69]

The "original men" would drive the devilish white men out of Asia and into Europe, where they reportedly lived a savage and uncivilized existence until the coming of Mussa, who taught the white devils what NOI calls "Tricknology."

Tricknology represents a generalized capacity by whites for deception and manipulation that is understood as nearly magical in nature and resulted in the enslavement of blacks. Central to Tricknology was the divorcing of blacks from their traditional religion of Islam (meaning Islam as understood by NOI). Similar to orthodox Islamic belief, however, NOI postulates that the historical Jesus preached its version of Islam, not Christianity.[70] The emphasis on Tricknology may also play a role in NOI's extensive reputation for virulent anti-Semitism, as Yacub and Mussa are the Arabized names of the Hebrew patriarch Jacob and prophet Moses, respectively.[71]

The result of NOI's "science"-based theology is a conception of the world where the spiritual (whether Islam or Christianity) directly impacts the physical, which is to say the genetic or racial. Through adoption of Christianity, "Black Muslims" (as they were alternatively known) were understood as being physically as well as spiritually corrupted. And through the knowledge imparted by Elijah Muhammad's NOI, this process could be reversed.

This materialist vision predicated on racial pseudoscience dominated not just NOI theology but also its praxis. Elijah Muhammad emphasized the physical health and welfare of NOI adherents, arguing that the secret knowledge of the black man's scientific superiority brought by Fard, together with a restorative program of personal and social health, could reverse the spiritual decay resulting from "six thousand years" of rule by Yacub's genetically created white devils. As Elijah Muhammad wrote in "Why They Urge You To Eat The Swine" from *Eat to Live*, a collected work of NOI's health and dietary commandments:

> Allah taught me that this grafted animal was made for medical purposes, not for a food for the people. That this animal destroys the beautiful appearance of its eaters. It takes away the shyness of those who eat this brazen flesh. Nature did not give the hog anything like shyness. Take a look at their immoral dress and actions; their worship of filthy songs and dances that an uncivilized animal or savage human being of the jungle cannot even imitate. Yet, average black people who want to be loved by their enemies, regardless of what God thinks of them, have gone to the extreme in trying to imitate the children of their slave masters in all of their wickedness, filthiness and evil.[72]

For Elijah Muhammad, you were literally what you ate, drank, or wore. This in turn was a part of NOI's social rehabilitation, as the Black

Muslims created a wide variety of restaurants, grocery and clothing stores, and every other manner of economic vehicle to meet the needs of the NOI faithful, separated from the corrupting influence of whites. By 1962, "the Nation owned apartments, office buildings, a construction company, a clothing factory and eventually, a bank. A farm in Michigan supplied its grocery stores, restaurants, and bakeries." All told, its enterprises were believed to be worth over $60 million, and Elijah Muhammad owned two mansions, one in Chicago (where NOI was based) and one in Phoenix.[73]

If W. D. Fard's second-in-command Elijah Muhammad was primarily responsible for crafting the NOI's theological message, then its political message was crafted by Muhammad's own lieutenant, Malcolm Little, a former gangster and bootlegger who converted to NOI in prison, got rid of his "slave" surname, and called himself Malcolm X.

Malcolm and the Nation

Malcolm X was in many ways a perfect complement to Elijah Muhammad.[74] Where Muhammad's speech was esoteric and confusing with an unimpressive delivery style, Malcolm X was known for fiery, impassioned rhetoric that resonated with the day-to-day lives of his audience.[75] From the 1950s to 1964, Malcolm X's leadership played a significant role in raising NOI's profile. Malcolm X's presentation eventually deemphasized the more difficult to swallow NOI teachings of god-scientists and genetically engineered white devils while still presenting a program of separation, self-rule, and self-defense.

Tension between Malcolm X and his rising political influence and Elijah Muhammad's rule over NOI had slowly been building, beginning with a disagreement over the NOI response to an April 1962 incident where a police stop of two Black Muslim men near a Los Angeles NOI mosque resulted in violence. When it was all over, six Black Muslims had been shot, one was killed, and numerous other injuries were reported—some from allegations of excessive force and abuse. A jury eventually ruled the shootings justified.[76]

Malcolm X immediately flew to Los Angeles to participate in a series of high-profile events and urged a violent response by NOI against the Los Angeles police. Elijah Muhammad demurred, possibly because of NOI's many valuable business interests in the city, and instead launched a propaganda offensive using NOI's newspaper *Muhammad Speaks* to focus on allegations of abuse and corruption surrounding the incident.[77]

Perhaps the best presentation of Malcolm X's views can be derived from his 1964 speech "The Ballot or the Bullet," given just after his departure from NOI. In it, Malcolm X outlined a program he identified as "black nationalism," which, while not couched in NOI's terminology, nonetheless evoked its core tenets of "scientific" self-improvement and social rehabilitation:

> The political philosophy of black nationalism means that the black man should control the politics and the politicians in his own community; no more. The black man in the black community has to be re-educated into the science of politics so he will know what politics is supposed to bring him in return. Don't be throwing out any ballots. A ballot is like a bullet. You don't throw your ballots until you see a target, and if that target is not within your reach, keep your ballot in your pocket....
>
> The economic philosophy of black nationalism is pure and simple. It only means that we should control the economy of our community. Why should white people be running all the stores in our community? Why should white people be running the banks of our community? Why should the economy of our community be in the hands of the white man? Why?

> If a black man can't move his store into a white community, you tell me why a white man should move his store into a black community. The philosophy of black nationalism involves a re-education program in the black community in regards to economics. Our people have to be made to see that any time you take your dollar out of your community and spend it in a community where you don't live, the community where you live will get poorer and poorer, and the community where you spend your money will get richer and richer....
>
> The social philosophy of black nationalism only means that we have to get together and remove the evils, the vices, alcoholism, drug addiction, and other evils that are destroying the moral fiber of our community. We ourselves have to lift the level of our community, the standard of our community to a higher level, make our own society beautiful so that we will be satisfied in our own social circles and won't be running around here trying to knock our way into a social circle where we're not wanted. So I say, in spreading a gospel such as black nationalism, it is not designed to make the black man re-evaluate the white man—you know him already—but to make the black man re-evaluate himself. Don't change the white man's mind—you can't change his mind, and that whole thing about appealing to the moral conscience of America—America's conscience is bankrupt. She lost all conscience a long time ago. Uncle Sam has no conscience.[78]

Malcolm X also sought to internationalize the black nationalist struggle in the context of other conflicts. The NOI pseudo-genetic conception of all races was no doubt of assistance as Malcolm X took inspiration from other conflicts ranging from the war against Japan in World War II to Vietnam:

> So the only place where action can take place is on the ground. And the white man can't win another war fighting on the ground. Those days are over. The black man knows it, the brown man knows it, the red man knows it, and the yellow man knows it. So they engage him in guerrilla warfare. That's not his style. You've got to have heart to be a guerrilla warrior, and he hasn't got any heart. I'm telling you now.[79]

This enabled Malcolm X to counter the appeal of the ongoing civil rights movement, which was couched in American terms of equality for all, and transition the discussion into international conflict, including decolonization:

> Uncle Sam's hands are dripping with blood, dripping with the blood of the black man in this country. He's the earth's number-one hypocrite. He has the audacity—yes, he has—imagine him posing as the leader of the free world. The free world! And you over here singing "We Shall Overcome." Expand the civil-rights struggle to the level of human rights. Take it into the United Nations, where our African brothers can throw their weight on our side, where our Asian brothers can throw their weight on our side, where our Latin-American brothers can throw their weight on our side, and where 800 million Chinamen are sitting there waiting to throw their weight on our side.[80]

This internationalization required abandoning NOI's aversion to identifying blacks in America with Africa, and the language of the "Asiatic black man" was cast aside:

> You're nothing but Africans. Nothing but Africans. In fact, you'd get farther calling yourself African instead of Negro. Africans don't catch hell. You're the only one catching hell. They don't have to pass civil-rights bills for Africans. An African can go anywhere he wants right now. All you've got to do is tie your head up. That's right, go anywhere you want. Just stop being a Negro.[81]

The split would widen further after Elijah Muhammad punished Malcolm X with a "suspension" for his now-infamous declaration that the assassination of President John F. Kennedy was the result of "chickens coming home to roost."[82] The feud intensified when Malcolm X revealed that Elijah Muhammad reportedly had illicit sexual relations with a number of young women who served as his personal secretaries, a response to NOI's attempt to evict Malcolm X from the apartment where he lived with his wife and children.[83] Malcolm X also accused Muhammad of siding with white supremacists—including, notably, George Lincoln Rockwell's American Nazi Party and the Ku Klux Klan (KKK)—in order to support a separate state for blacks in the rural south.[84] Various members of NOI were forced to choose sides as Malcolm X launched his own group, Muslim Mosque, Inc., and faced repeated threats from Elijah Muhammad supporters, including the firebombing of his apartment.[85]

Malcolm X eventually abandoned NOI's theology altogether and converted to orthodox Sunni Islam before founding the Organization of Afro-American Unity (OAAU) to further his black nationalist political agenda. But before the OAAU became a truly viable and independent organization, Malcolm X was assassinated on February 21, 1965, by several men believed to NOI supporters armed with a sawed-off shotgun and semi-automatic pistols. Thomas Hagen (also known as Talmadge X Hayer) confessed to the killing, admitting it was done to avenge what was seen as insults by Malcolm X against Elijah Muhammad. Hayer denied that two alleged accomplices, Thomas Johnson and Norman

3X Butler (later known as Muhammad Abdul Aziz), were involved. All three men were convicted, but the convictions of Johnson and Butler were overturned and officially expunged in November 2021.[86]

After Malcolm

The murder of Malcolm X could not reverse the fracturing of NOI. At the same time Malcolm X was rebelling against Elijah Muhammad, another schismatic figure, Clarence 13X, emerged. Clarence 13X (real name Clarence Edward Smith), left NOI, disputing the central claim that W. D. Fard was in fact God in the flesh. Instead, Clarence 13X, styling himself Allah the Father, drew from some NOI tracts to postulate that all black men were "Gods" in his founding of the "Five Percenters," also known as the Nation of Gods and Earths.

According to the FBI, Clarence 13X's appeal reached a number of Harlem-based street gangs, who liked the relaxed strictures compared to Elijah Muhammad's NOI, referring to themselves as "the five percent" of NOI adherents who "believe in smoking and drinking."[87] Since the organization's founding in 1965, the "Five Percenters" have largely styled themselves a "culture" rather than a religious belief system, while law enforcement and correction officials have traditionally viewed the group as racial supremacist prison gang.[88]

Elijah Muhammad's son, Wallace D. Muhammad (also known as Warith Deen Muhammad or W. Deen Muhammad), like Malcolm X, grew increasingly rebellious against the traditional NOI theology imposed by his father. He left or was expelled from the organization multiple times. He eventually took power in 1974 with the death of Elijah Muhammad and began to move NOI onto the path of orthodox Sunni Islam charted by Malcolm X.[89] Under Wallace Muhammad, , NOI adopted the name Muslim American Society, now known as Mosque Cares.

Not every NOI adherent accepted the change. Most famously, Louis Farrakhan created the newspaper *The Final Call* to replace the old

Muhammad Speaks outlet. Farrakhan used this platform to reinstitute NOI under its original theology, basing this remnant out of NOI's long-time headquarters in Chicago.[90]

Farrakhan, born as Louis Eugene Walcott, had been recruited into NOI in 1955 after a successful career as a calypso singer under the name Calypso Gene.[91] Farrakhan had been a close associate of Malcolm X but supported Elijah Muhammad during the split. There have long been allegations that Farrakhan played a role in the assassination of Malcolm X. While Farrakhan has maintained that he did not order the killing, he has admitted that his rhetoric, including calling Malcolm X a "traitor" "deserving of death," created an atmosphere that played a role.[92]

Farrakhan continued to maintain that W. D. Fard was in fact God in the flesh and that Elijah Muhammad was a unique prophet of God. In presentations Farrakhan declared that Elijah Muhammad took him up in a UFO (referred to as the Mother Wheel) and supplied him with unique prophecies about a future cataclysmic conflict between NOI and the United States.[93] Farrakhan also considerably amplified the ideological anti-Semitism of NOI under his leadership such that most NOI critics came to identify NOI principally for its anti-Semitic rather than its racial supremacist doctrine.[94]

Even so, under Farrakhan's leadership, NOI increasingly received a level of mainstream recognition, particularly among celebrity and political circles, beginning with the 1995 Million Man March, where Farrakhan shared arcane rhetoric[95] with the audience of some half a million people and the stage with notable icons such as Rosa Parks, Maya Angelou, Jesse Jackson, Al Sharpton, then-chairman of the Black Congressional Caucus Donald Payne, and D.C. Mayor Marion Barry.[96] The success of the Million Man March resulted in its being repeated in the Millions More Movement March in 2005 and as the increasingly combative "Justice or Else" march in 2015.

The endorsement by notable politicians and celebrities has resulted in an increased appeal of NOI rhetoric. While the total number of NOI official adherents remains relatively low—estimated at between

20,000 and 50,000 members—the adoption of partial elements of the group's rhetoric and beliefs may become increasingly commonplace.

Nation of Islam and Law Enforcement

Fruit of Islam

Despite its ideology grounded in pseudoscience and racial hatred against whites, as the assassination of Malcolm X highlights, historically many NOI victims have themselves been black.

Many NOI members were subjected to what Elijah Muhammad's son Wallace called NOI's "'punch-your-teeth-out' squad" known as the Fruit of Islam.[97] A paramilitary organization known for its unique blue uniforms and hats, the Fruit of Islam in theory represented a unique training program directed toward all male adherents of the NOI, but in practice it represented Elijah Muhammad's corps of bodyguards and enforcers who upheld the leader's will and executed punishments for violations of NOI's social and moral code.

Under Farrakhan, the Fruit of Islam also became big business, as NOI organized a number of "security agencies" consisting of Fruit of Islam members to provide security at public housing sites, making millions in government contracts in the 1990s.[98] Supporters of NOI's security forces, which according to the *New York Times* included "many black politicians," argued that NOI was able to calm tensions, prevent crimes, and push out drug dealers in ways that the police could not:

> Still, the guards from the Nation of Islam, who have been called to clean up crack-infested streets and protect black politicians and celebrities, wield a weapon that often eludes the police in black neighborhoods: respect.

> "They are more effective than police," said Spike Lee, the film director, who has used members of the Nation of Islam to guard his sets for movies, including "Do the Right Thing," "Jungle Fever" and "Malcolm X."
>
> "The police and black people have never gotten along," he said, "and the community just has great respect for the Nation of Islam."[99]

NOI routinely used security forces for plausible deniability, considering them independent entities when press was bad but a vital part of NOI's outreach when media was more positive. According to the ADL however, the various security agencies were made up of overlapping leadership consisting almost entirely of high-level NOI leaders who were personally close to Farrakhan himself:

> While on paper the security companies are separate corporate entities, the firms appear thoroughly intertwined with the Nation of Islam itself, sharing officers, direction and control. Nation of Islam officials themselves have implied that Farrakhan and his lieutenants exert controlling influence over the companies, and that income may be upstreamed to Louis Farrakhan. The president of N.O.I. Security has denounced critics of the firm as "people who are seeking to deny financial benefits ... to Minister Farrakhan."[100]

According to the ADL, NOI security firms had a reputation for "securing" communities with over-the-top violence bordering on vigilantism and tolerated drug dealing even while intimidating innocent civilians and attacking police.[101]

In addition to top-down violence directed to enforce NOI's strictures, there has also been Muslim-on-Muslim violence as a result of competition over NOI's lucrative businesses and properties and over territory for proselytizing. In some cases, violence surrounded criminal enterprises such as drug trafficking—whether to eliminate it in Black Muslim–controlled neighborhoods or merely to control it for additional profit. Peele describes, for example, the conflict between the Oakland and San Francisco Nation Mosques that resulted in the murder of nine Bay Area Black Muslims in 1971 and 1972:

> Whether Joseph Stephens [aka Yusuf Ali Bey] intended to take over their territory to profit for himself or drive them away has never been fully known. What is known is that a notorious Oakland hitman, "Friendly" Freddy Payne, joined Mosque 26B and was soon executing other Muslims. At 10:15 p.m. on November 14, 1971, Payne and two other men burst into the East Oakland home of Bill Mapp, a drug dealer who, like Payne, had recently become a Muslim but not abandoned his line of work. Mapp wasn't there, but his wife was, along with another Muslim named al-Rashid, who was visiting from Oregon. He drew a .38 caliber pistol and began firing at Payne. The intruders shot back, killing him. They fled down a hall where Mapp's eight-year-old daughter Kimberly, slept in an alcove. As she sat up in bed as the gunmen raced by, one of them shot her in the face, killing her instantly.
>
> Just three nights earlier, a Muslim husband and wife living nearby had died in an attack that bore strong similarities to the murders of Wendell and Birdie Mae Scott: Someone kicked in their door, shot them in their bed, took nothing, and fled, leaving a relative alive in a different bedroom.
>
> All of the victims were members of either Mosque 26

or Mosque 26B– except for Al-Rashid and another Muslim killed in San Francisco who was from Chicago, perhaps sent as a peacemaker.[102]

Yusuf Ali Bey later split from NOI and, while maintaining its ideology to run his criminal enterprise out of *Your Black Muslim Bakery* in Oakland, became a fixture of the city and ran for Oakland mayor. The outfit he established, which would be run by his descendants, launched a reign of terror that included kidnapping, rape and sexual abuse, and outright murder lasting from 1971 until 2011, when Yusuf Ali Bey IV was convicted of the 2007 murder of black Oakland journalist Chauncey Bailey, who was doing a story on the group.[103]

In many historical cases, it can be difficult to determine where violence from criminal enterprise ended and ideological violence began. Philadelphia's Black Muslim Mafia (alternatively Black Mafia or Muslim Mafia) engaged in racketeering, narcotics trafficking, extortion, armed robbery, and murder-for-hire in Philadelphia from 1969 until about 1980. One of its leading members, Sam Christian (also known as Suleiman Bey), was also a captain in the local chapter of the Fruit of Islam following the gang's merger with the local Nation Mosque apparatus. Other members of the gang played senior roles in the Fruit as well, conducting security screenings and vetting new members. Membership in NOI was an important factor in gang leadership. The gang was said to provide $4,000 a month to the mosque as a "tribute" by 1973, and the mosque shielded the gang from legal scrutiny.[104]

But the gang is most infamous for the January 1973 "Hanafi murders," which shocked the nation at the time. Black Muslim Mafia members killed seven people—two adults and five children—in the home of basketball legend and orthodox Muslim convert Kareem Abdul-Jabbar. Author Sean Patrick Griffin writes:

> The slayings revolved around an ideological dispute between the Black Muslims and the Hanafi aka Sunni sect of Muslims. The intended target was

> Hamaas Abdul Khaalis, leader of the 1,000-member Washington sect of Hanafis. On January 5th, Khaalis sent a letter to Black Muslim ministers denouncing the Black Muslims and Elijah Muhammad as "false prophets." In the opening paragraph, he called Elijah Muhammad a "lying deceiver." Khaalis also wrote a similar letter in December 1972 and sent both letters to 58 mosques nationwide.[105]

The brutal slayings were done to avenge the honor of Elijah Muhammad, although at least some of the gang members may have believed the raid was intended to be a heist.

Hamaas Abdul Khaalis was a former NOI member who had converted to the Hanafi school of orthodox Sunni Islam. The incident kicked off a series of retaliatory actions beginning the following day, when four Muslim men took hostages at John and Al's Sporting Goods store in what they later said was an attempt to steal firearms to defend against expected NOI attacks.[106] Khaalis himself, in March 1977, launched a hostage taking of his own, demanding justice for the 1973 killings, even though the perpetrators had been convicted and faced significant prison sentences.[107]

Certainly not all violence with a link to NOI ideology was black-on-black, however. From 1973 to 1976, San Francisco suffered through the "Zebra Murders," a series of grisly black-on-white murders.

"When people talk about Zebra, it's usually as a serial killing. That may be technically true, but the most accurate description of what Zebra was is terrorism, plain and simple," according to Earl Sanders, one of the police officers who investigated the case.[108]

Police suspected early on that the killings were racially motivated and linked to the NOI local chapter Mosque #26,[109] but they struggled to find sources inside NOI.[110] Ultimately 23 people were attacked and 15 people were murdered, all but two of them by firearm. Some sources say additional related ideological killings went unsolved as well.[111] The perpetrators were later identified as Jessie Lee Cooks, Larry Craig

Green, Manuel Moore, and J. C. X. Simon—four NOI members—after a fifth member of the group, Anthony Harris, received a reward and immunity from prosecution to testify against them.[112]

All of the perpetrators were linked to Black Self Help Storage, an NOI-linked business, and were identified as members of the "Death Angels," an offshoot of the Fruit of Islam security force.[113] In Clark Howard's exhaustive book on the killings entitled *Zebra*, the Death Angels are described as an "elite" group within the Fruit of Islam, with the requirement for membership including the killing of four white people.[114] Such beliefs may go back all the way to the founding of NOI under W. D. Fard, with one early NOI pamphlet, "The Secret Rituals of the Lost-Found Nation of Islam," stating: "Every man of Islam must gain a victory over the devil. Four victories and a son gains his reward." That pamphlet was found near the body of the man killed in the ritual murder that forced W. D. Fard to flee Detroit in the 1930s.[115]

While NOI officially denied any connection to the incident, it provided attorneys for three of the perpetrators who sought a jury trial. (Cooks pled guilty.)[116] All four men were convicted and received long sentences.

According to reports, the attacks may also have been a response to a police-involved shooting of a Black Muslim following a traffic stop days before the first murder. If true, the "Zebra" killings can be seen as a reflection of the violence once threatened by Malcolm X in response to the 1962 Los Angeles police shooting incident mentioned earlier—this time apparently without Elijah Muhammad's call for restraint.

Nation of Islam and Violence Against Police

Clashes between NOI and police were not uncommon—and often politically charged. Perhaps the most notorious example is the so-called 1972 Harlem Mosque Incident, in which police officer Phillip Cardillo was murdered by an unknown member of NOI while he and his partner responded to a 10-13 "officer in need of assistance" call

Kyle Shideler

from Nation of Islam Mosque #7, run by Louis Farrakhan. The *Queens Gazette* described the situation as it occurred April 14, 1972:

> At 11:41 a.m. on that fateful day, a call was made to 911 by a "Detective Thomas of the 28th Precinct" reporting a 10-13 at 102 West 116th St. in Harlem. The address turned out to be the location of Mosque Number 7, headed by Minister Louis Farrakhan. Responding to the call was Cardillo, accompanied by his partner, Vito Navarra. Two additional officers, Victor Padilla and Ivan Negron, arrived at the mosque the same moment.
>
> The four patrolmen, believing that one of their fellow officers was in trouble, entered the mosque. Once inside they found the place to be eerily silent and abandoned. They quickly came face to face with dozens and dozens of members of the Fruit of Islam. Two metal doors were suddenly closed behind them and Cardillo, Navarra, Padilla and Negron were trapped. The call about a 10-13 was fake. It was bait used to lure them in. As other officers, including [Detective Randy] Jurgensen, who was on a stakeout nearby, rushed to the scene to help the "officer" in trouble, the cries of Cardillo and his men could be heard coming over the police radios. Now there really was a situation. The officers were beaten severely and their guns were taken from them. Powerless and outnumbered, all they could do was try to survive until help arrived. Officer Rudy Andre arrived at the scene, entered the mosque, and found the four men being brutally beaten. Unable to get through the doors that were bolted from the inside, Andre took his gun and fired through the small glass window in the door sending the attackers scattering in all directions and in the process severing a major

artery in his arm. When it was all over, Navarra, Padilla and Negron lay severely beaten with mutilated faces and Cardillo, stripped of his firearm, was shot at point blank range and died six days later on April 20.[117]

The situation rapidly escalated as the mosque was soon surrounded by an angry crowd of some 750-1000 people, and individuals on top of the mosque rained down glass bottles and other dangerous objects onto policemen attempting to secure the outside perimeter so an investigation could take place inside. The situation was further aggravated by the arrival of Farrakhan, accompanied by U.S. Congressman Charlie Rangel, founding member of the Congressional Black Caucus. Rangel and Farrakhan persuaded on-scene commanders to reduce the exterior police perimeter to ease tensions by removing white police officers. When the situation predictably escalated, they subsequently urged police to abandon the crime scene entirely and vacate the mosque, promising to bring suspects to the precinct for further questioning, which never occurred. Inexplicably, police officers who were also NOI members were allowed to speak to suspects, both at the mosque and later at the police precinct. These actions ultimately resulted in loss of control of the crime scene and permanently hobbled future attempts at an investigation.[118]

Eventually prosecutors charged Louis 17X Dupree, a high-ranking NOI official at the mosque, for the crime based on identification by the assaulted officers, but after an initial mistrial, a second jury found the suspect not guilty.[119]

The originator of the 10-13 call was never determined, and questions have swirled about the provoking incident itself. One theory, posited by Detective Jurgensen, who investigated the case, is that the 10-13 was a "pretext call," a practice initiated by the FBI as part of the organization's now infamous "COINTELPRO" effort, one element of which was directed at black identity extremists. The FBI used pretext calls as a "counterintelligence" tactic intended to sow dissension within suspected radical organizations such as NOI, the

Black Panthers, the KKK, and other subversive organizations.[120]

Regardless of the FBI's practices, the use of fake emergency calls to bait ambushes for police was at the time, and remains today, a common tactic.

Almost a year earlier, the Black Liberation Army ambushed and murdered Officers Joseph A. Piagentini and Waverly Jones after luring them to a public housing project with an emergency call. More about the Black Liberation Army and this incident will be discussed in a later chapter.

As Detective Jurgensen noted, several elements suggest that the incident may have been a setup:

> "Somebody in authority had to order the guards off the doors of the mosque and leave them unlocked and unguarded," he said. "And somebody with knowledge of police procedure and personnel had to make that 10-13 call" sending the NYPD to the mosque.[121]

An examination of the aftermath of the ambush is useful from the perspective of assessing motive. NOI, and several political leaders with strong ties to it, began an immediate campaign to exploit the mosque incident to their advantage. Farrakhan demanded, and received, an apology from NYPD brass for the police violating the sanctity of NOI's place of worship. Deputy Commissioner Benjamin Ward issued an apology at a rally held at the mosque held the same night as the attack and publicly criticized the decision of officers to enter the mosque.[122]

In press accounts, Farrakhan described the incident as a premediated attack, which he compared to the "Bay of Pigs," while falsely claiming police were armed with "machine guns." He also claimed that NOI had a verbal agreement with previous police precinct leadership not to enter the mosque, which was not being upheld by the current police commander.[123] The precinct leadership claimed that they had an agreement only to treat the mosque as they would any other religious institution.[124] In addition to demanding special privileges for the mosque, NOI pushed for an "all-black police force" to patrol Harlem, with Farrakhan calling the effort to remove white officers from the area a "paramount issue:"

> About 5,000 blacks gathered in a Harlem armory yesterday and demonstrated their support for a Black Muslim demand that all white policemen in Harlem be replaced by "re-educated" black policemen. They cheered and applauded over and over again when Muslim Minister Louis Farrakhan denounced the "crimes" of white people that had led to the decision "to organize this black community" around the issue of Harlem being patrolled by "black officers commanded by black commanders accountable to the black community."[125]

Two months later, in June 1972, Deputy Commissioner Ward told an audience of the National Society of Afro-American Policemen, an organization largely consisting of Black Muslim police officers, that "the time is now to get your followers ready to move into these positions of power in this community."[126]

Police leadership ultimately rejected calls to transfer white police officers,[127] but they did institute a policy for "sensitive sites" linked to NOI, the Black Panther Party, and similar groups.[128] That policy remained in effect for more than 20 years.[129]

The Harlem Mosque incident should thus be viewed as part of an operational cycle of provocation, ambush, escalation, and subsequent propaganda aimed at furthering an explicit NOI policy of denying law enforcement access to their facilities and as part of an effort to gain control over the neighborhood by expelling white police and replacing them with NOI-aligned adherents. While such tactics are uncommon to strictly criminal organizations, they are easily recognizable hallmarks of subversion and insurgency tactics.

More than two decades later, the exact same cycle was repeated a week after touch-on-crime former Attorney General Rudy Giuliani took over as New York mayor. Once again, a false 911 call lured police officers to the same mosque, where they were ambushed on the stairs in the exact same way, deprived of their duty weapons, and beaten. Again, NOI and its allies sought political concessions, as *New York Magazine* describes:

> Onto the scene came Al Sharpton and his then-consigliere, C. Vernon Mason, who denounced the police for conducting a "siege" against a place of worship. The story whipped its way through the papers for the next few days, building and building. Sharpton, Mason, and other black leaders kept up the vitriol on their end, demanding an audience. Giuliani and Police Commissioner William Bratton weren't exactly shrinking violets either, with Giuliani chiding Room 9 reporters for paying too much attention to Sharpton. Things were, maybe, calming down. But when the NOI leaders showed up with Sharpton and Mason in tow, Giuliani and Bratton abruptly canceled the meetings. "I remember the moment very well," says Randy Mastro, the deputy mayor for operations at the time. "Rudy said, 'No, I'm not going to meet with Al Sharpton, and my police commissioner is not going to meet with Al Sharpton.'" The NOI leaders came back the next day. They got their meetings.[130]

Nation of Islam and State Sponsors of Terrorism

NOI had extensive interaction with several state supporters of terrorism, most notoriously, although not exclusively, with Libya's Muammar Qaddafi. Under Qaddafi, from 1973 to the early 1990s, Libya provided weapons and training to a wide variety of terrorist groups—

from the Provisional Irish Republican Army to Palestinian Marxist terror group the Popular Front for the Liberation of Palestine (PFLP) and others—and actively sponsored terror attacks.[131]

Beginning in 1985, a financial relationship developed between Libya and NOI when the Libyan Islamic Call Society, a Libyan state charity known to finance terrorists, provided a $5 million "loan" to NOI, allegedly for the creation of a hair-care business.[132]

The Islamic Call Society was directly linked to Qaddafi and dominated by Libya's intelligence services. One of its purposes was to help Qaddafi circumvent increasing U.S. sanctions while supporting the various terrorist and rebel networks the Libyan regime supported, including NOI.[133]

Qaddafi reportedly also offered NOI "a huge shipment of arms," which Farrakhan claimed to have rejected.[134] In 1996, Qaddafi reportedly offered NOI a billion dollars to influence U.S. elections and foreign policy. Qaddafi called NOI a "breach" in the American "fortress."[135] Clinton administration officials eventually stepped up to block the deal.[136]

During the 2011 U.S. intervention in Libya, Farrakhan remained a loyal supporter of the embattled Libyan dictator, condemning the U.S. military action and Qaddafi's eventual killing by U.S.-backed rebels.[137]

While there is no indication that NOI ever committed terrorism on behalf of Qaddafi, the group was linked to the El Rukns, the MSTA-devoted street gang that did face charges for a prospective terrorist plot on behalf of Qaddafi. Farrakhan called the El Rukns "divine warriors" and may have been responsible for introducing them to his Libyan contacts.[138] According to an El Rukn member turned government witness, Farrakhan's ministers also received shipments of cocaine from the gang in exchange for possible entry into NOI's empire of legitimate businesses.[139]

Other known state sponsors of terrorism with historic links to NOI included the Sudanese regime of Omar Bashir, as the ADL writes:

Farrakhan's contacts with other outlaw states are less well known. The NOI leader visited Khartoum in 1994, where he met with Gen. Omar Hassan Ahmed al-Bashir, the Sudanese head of state and Dr. Hassan Abdullah al-Turabi, who heads The Sudan's ruling party, and is the power behind the throne. Farrakhan's party included his chief of staff, Leonard Farrakhan Muhammad, who heads the New Life Self-Development security company in Chicago, and Farrakhan's son, Assistant Supreme Captain Mustapha Farrakhan, who is a consultant to N.O.I. Security Agency Inc. in Washington. The younger Farrakhan is also deputy to N.O.I. Security Agency president William/Abdul Sharrieff Muhammad, in the latter's role as Supreme Captain of the Fruit of Islam.[140]

Members of NOI also attended the Popular Arab Islamic Conferences, held in Sudan throughout the 1990s, with numerous terrorist groups in attendance including Hezbollah, Hamas, and Al Qaeda's Osama bin Laden.

NOI's affiliation with terrorist states continues to more recent years as well, with Farrakhan traveling to Iran in 2018, where he appeared on Iranian state television and led students in a "Death to America" and "Death to Israel" chant.[141] Such language is concerning from a group that described itself as "the Hezbollah of America," a reference to the Iranian-backed Lebanese Shia terrorist group.[142]

Except for the El Rukn–Gaddafi plot, most of NOI's interactions with foreign states represent a subversive rather than a terrorist threat. Attacks by NOI supporters are typically disavowed by the group as a whole or committed by individuals motivated by NOI's black supremacist ideology, but there is little or no evidence of direct orchestration by the group itself.

The murder of a U.S. Capitol Police officer in April 2021 by 25-year-old NOI supporter Noah Green is an example of this kind of attack:

> Police say Green rammed a dark-colored sedan into a security barrier outside the U.S. Capitol, killing Officer William "Billy" Evans, an 18-year veteran of the U.S. Capitol Police Department. After the crash, police say, Green got out of the car with a knife in his hand, ran toward officers and ignored their commands. Officers opened fire and killed him.[143]

Acquaintances described the West Virginia–born Green as a "quiet, athletic, non-violent" person who in the years prior to the attack had undergone a series of personality changes. A few months prior to the attack Green moved to Botswana for reasons that remain unclear.[144]

Green's social media was increasingly filled with references to NOI, and Green described himself as a "Follower of Farrakhan." Green's last social media post included references to an end-times prophecy by Elijah Muhammad.[145]

For their part, NOI leaders largely disavowed Green, blaming the attack on mental illness, although they did admit that he had been studying to attain membership prior to the attack.[146]

Nation of Islam

> Founder: W. D. Fard
> Established: 1930 in Detroit
> Notable Members: Elijah Muhammad, Malcolm X, Muhammad Ali, Louis Farrakhan
> Summary of Ideology: blames Christianity as a false religion that deliberately divorced blacks from their original religious identity as Muslims to enable their enslavement by whites, racial supremacy grounded in "science," a sort of mirror-image of the Darwinian or eugenic racism common at the time of NOI's founding
> Subgroups: Black Muslim Mafia, Fruit of Islam, Death Angels
> Estimated Adherents: 20,000 to 50,000
> Distinguishing Practices: black suits and bowties for NOI males, blue

uniform and cap for Fruit of Islam members, logo of a white crescent with a white star on a red background

SECTION TWO: BLACK SEPARATISM, MARXISM, AND BLACK LIBERATION

Aleksandr Viktorovich Ionov, a Russian national and head of the "Anti-Globalization Movement" based in Moscow, was indicted by the U.S. Department of Justice (DOJ) in the summer of 2022. Ionov, DOJ alleged, operated as an agent of Russia's state security agency, the FSB, when he coordinated and funded two black separatist organizations. Those two groups were the African People's Socialist Party (APSP), also known as the Uhuru Movement, which campaigned and ran candidates for local offices on a platform of demanding reparations from white Americans, and an APSP splinter group known as the Black Hammers, which had previously been the focus of international news for an attempt to set up an autonomous black homeland in the mountains in Colorado.[147]

While the total dollar amounts and political impact of these campaigns were probably negligible, the case serves as a reminder that, as this author noted when the Ionov indictment was issued, "For nearly a century, the Russian intelligence services have sought to exploit grievances among African-Americans, to penetrate and manipulate mainstream civil rights movements, and to provoke extremism within black communities."[148]

Almost immediately following the successful 1917 Russian Revolution and the subsequent civil war, the victorious Soviets formed the Comintern (Communist International) to organize international efforts at fomenting revolution within the homelands of their capitalist opponents. Following the direction of first Vladimir Lenin and later his successor Josef Stalin, the Comintern had a particular emphasis on fomenting revolution among the black population of the United States. Michael Wojnowski of the Warsaw Institute writes:

> The plan of using African Americans for the Kremlin's geopolitical agenda was authored by Nikolai Nasonov (1902–1938), a member of the Russian Communist Party (Bolsheviks) and the head of the Negro Bureau at the Eastern Secretariat. The Bureau was established on December 25, 1928, and was transformed into the Negro Section at the Eastern Secretariat in September 1929. It focused on matters concerning the life of Black people in the United States and colonies. It also conducted propaganda and agitation work. In his article The Negro Problem in the United States of America, which was published in August 1928, Nasonov made a geopolitical, economic, military, and demographic assessment of Soviet foreign policy. He wrote African Americans could be a tool for fomenting the situation in the United States while inspiring the situation in colonies. According to him, the Black population of the Black Belt should be considered a "nation" to eventually create a "national liberation movement" to undermine American imperialism. Nasonov pointed to Joseph Stalin's definition of nation in his major work Marxism and the National Question, saying agitation and propaganda efforts should rely upon the Leninist interpretation of the right to self-determination, or the right to political independence. It was the nation's "full right to secession," preceded by a nationwide referendum.[149]

The Comintern's principal tool was the Communist Party USA (CPUSA), which fully devoted itself to fulfilling the Comintern's directive to foment separatism and revolt with an emphasis on the Southern "black belt" where the majority of the African American population of the time lived. Wojnowski described how the CPUSA was

> advised to bring together Communist party structures, trade unions, and abolitionist organizations in the South to eventually stage an armed revolution that the CPUSA deemed most efficient for achieving political goals. Earl Russell Browder (1891–1973), the leader of the CPUSA, agreed with that, saying Black people of the Black Belt could only be liberated by toppling the regime of White landlords and capitalists. The Resolution of October 30, 1930, called for immediate measures for the organization of "proletarian and peasant self-defense" against the Ku-Klux-Klan. Comintern leaders paradoxically found it useful for provocations staged by clandestine structures and Soviet intelligence services, as read in the resolution: "Even some relatively insignificant acts of the Ku-Klux-Klan bandits in the Black Belt can become the occasion of important political movements, provided the Communists can organize the resistance of the indignant Negro masses."[150]

Such provocations and organized responses may have played some role in the 1919 Red Summer, a series of ugly and lethal nationwide race riots that began after the shooting of a white deputy sheriff outside a black union meeting in Elaine, Arkansas.[151] Notable in the 1919 Red Summer was the involvement of the African Blood Brotherhood for African Liberation and Redemption, a Communist organization that represented the first historical effort of "armed self-defense" by a black radical organization.

The program overtly praised the Soviet Union, emphasized a Pan-African connection to the continent, and compared the status of

American blacks with those in African colonies abroad. The program proposed acquiring arms and constructing "great Pan-African army in the same way as the Sinn Fein built up the Irish Army under the very nose of England."[152]

The appropriate role of arms in black liberation as well as the appropriateness of images and expectations of Pan-African unity remain significant questions among black identity extremists to the present day.

Stalin personally officiated at a 1929 Comintern meeting that directed the CPUSA to act on "the Negro question," support a "national Negro liberation movement," and establish a "Negro Soviet Republic" in the southern United States through subversion and violence. "In those regions of the South in which compact Negro masses are living, it is essential to put forward the slogan of the 'Right to Self-Determination for Negroes,'" a Comintern thesis on "The Revolutionary Movement in the Colonies" stated. "A radical transformation of the agrarian structure of the Southern States is one of the basic tasks of the revolution. Negro Communists must explain to non-Negro workers and peasants that only their close union with the white proletariat and joint struggle with them against the American bourgeoisie can lead to their liberation from barbarous exploitation and that only the victorious proletarian revolution will completely and permanently solve the agrarian and national questions of the Southern United States in the interests of the overwhelming majority of the Negro population of the country," the Comintern thesis said, with a letter instructing the CPUSA to comply.[153]

The Soviets' extensive efforts to recruit, indoctrinate, and train "Negro Communists" as part of their "divisive operations" against the United States came at the same time the black community struggled to establish its role and identity within American society. Communism became the ideological framework for numerous leading black intellectuals, including author Langston Hughes, poet Claude McKay, NAACP founder W. E. B. DuBois (who joined the CPUSA later in life), and author James Baldwin, among others.[154]

Soviet propagandists assiduously courted these black intellectuals, and a number of them made highly publicized trips to the Soviet Union. Mike Gonzalez notes that, in 1932, Langston Hughes "was one of 23 black Americans to go to Moscow to help make a Soviet propaganda film about race and labor relations in the American South. The artists had been recruited by Louise Thompson, the African American founder of the Harlem branch of the Friends of the Soviet Union."[155] Hughes went on to serve as the president of the Communist-linked League of Struggle for Negro Rights.

It should be noted that during this period, numerous American intellectuals of every race succumbed to, and perpetuated, Soviet propaganda. But Soviet agitation came at a significant time for the nascent black intellectual and civic life.

Despite success among black intellectuals, Soviet propaganda proved less impactful in its efforts to create Communist-led black mass movement organizations, particularly among labor unions, and overall CPUSA membership by black rank-and-file remained low. As the FBI's 1956 report "The Communist Party and the Negro" noted in its summary:

> The Communist Party USA, despite its concentrated efforts, has failed to attract even a significant minority of Negroes in the United States to its program. While it attempts to practice its policy of agitation and propaganda among the negroes on a nationwide basis, the majority of its attention is devoted to Negroes living in the Southern States.... At present time it can be stated that along with the decline in the national membership of the Communist Party, USA, the Party has experienced an increasingly greater decline, percentage wise, in its Negro membership.[156]

Others argue, however, that simply identifying black membership in the CPUSA is not a useful measurement of the impact Communist organizers had on the black community in the Soviet-targeted "black belt." As Professor Robin Kelley, author of *The Hammer and the Hoe: Alabama Communists During the Great Depression*, told *NPR*:

> Well, there's a couple of ways to think about this. One, in terms of actual dues-paying members, they never had more than 600, 700. But then, if you look at all the other auxiliary organizations, the International Labor Defense, which focused on civil rights issues, they had up to 2,000. The Sharecroppers Union had up to 12,000. You had the International Workers Order. You had the League of Young Southerners. You had the Southern Negro Youth Congress. If you add up all these organizations, it touched the lives easily of 20,000 people.[157]

Moving into the 1950s, Soviet efforts to create a Communist mass movement for American blacks and promote a separatist black national homeland in the deep South gave way to seeking to exploit what the FBI itself called the "legitimate grievances" of black Americans, most notably Jim Crow laws in the South.[158] A select number of the controlled Communist cadres worked for decades to infiltrate, influence, and take control of mainstream African American and civil rights organizations. This effort was itself part of a worldwide Comintern shift to Popular Front organizing, which emphasized operating within and among other socialist and even liberal groups as a means of advancing the Communist cause rather than building independent Communist groups. The focus exploited American racial tensions and struggles over civil rights as a propaganda club with which the Soviets could oppose U.S. efforts globally, especially in Africa, and not solely as an attempt to stoke violent revolution within the United States itself.

At the same time, support for the Soviets among American Communists began to wane after the release of Nikita Khrushchev's secret speech of 1956, in which he denounced Stalin, who had died three years before, and laid blame for all abuses and atrocities on him personally. The "Red Diaper babies" of Communist Party parents—those who came of age in the 1960s and '70s—found the existing Soviet-style CPUSA stodgy and restrictive and came to identify themselves as the "New Left."

After Fidel Castro seized power in Cuba in 1959, the Soviets saw an opportunity to challenge America in its own hemisphere, and the KGB directly trained Cuban intelligence. The New Left was in awe of Castro and especially charismatic guerrilla leader Che Guevera, and subsequently most Soviet Bloc efforts to influence the United States were undertaken through Cuban proxies. This paralleled the momentum of the decolonization movement against Britain, Belgium, France, and other European powers and the re-animation of new black identity movements in Africa and the Caribbean. Teishan Latner argues that Cuba was the "most consistent foreign influence on left wing radicalism in the U.S." and that the example of the Cuban Revolution particularly influenced black American leftists.[159]

The role of Communist organizing in the American civil rights movement is a touchy one. On the one hand, invoking the role of Communist organizers—the most important of whom were mainly white—was viewed by many at the time, and is still viewed now, as an attempt to minimize or ignore genuine issues of race relations and civil rights in the United States. On the other hand, in more triumphalist moments, those supportive of these same Communists organizers applaud the central role party members played in many of the most significant events of the era. A quote from the self-identified socialist magazine *Jacobin* suffices as an example: "Today is the 59th anniversary of the March on Washington, so get ready for plenty of whitewashed history. Here's the truth: the Civil Rights Movement was a radical struggle against Jim Crow tyranny whose early foot soldiers were Communists and labor militants."[160]

Because of Soviet intelligence covert operations in exploiting American racial tensions, measures against them were considered a counterintelligence responsibility, as a principal purpose of counterintelligence is to neutralize hostile foreign intelligence services. It was President John F. Kennedy and his brother, Attorney General Robert F. Kennedy, who directed FBI Director J. Edgar Hoover to wiretap the Reverend Martin Luther King Jr. as part of an effort to persuade him to separate himself from professional Soviet agents who had gained his confidence. The Kennedys instructed the FBI to take simultaneous aggressive action in the South against the KKK. That effort led to scandalous and criminal abuses under a series of years-long FBI operations called Counterintelligence Programs, or COINTELPRO.

What is important to understand is the impact these long running Soviet bloc efforts, working through the CPUSA and other Communist organizations, had to promote narratives of separatism and armed revolution, with the collateral effect of provoking federal law enforcement to break the law and discredit itself.

The themes of promoting illegal separatism and violence remained central to black power and black liberation organizations that arose during the 1960s and early 1970s and in turn serve as models and inspirations for several present-day BIE groups.

Chapter Three:
Black Panthers

Formation and Ideology

The Black Panther Party for Self Defense (BPPSD)—with its snarling panther logo and uniform of black leather jackets, berets, and open-carried rifles and shotguns—was at the time, and remains today, one of the most iconic images of the revolutionary milieu of the 1960s and '70s. Huey P. Newton and Bobby Seale formed the BPPSD in 1966.[161]

Huey Percy Newton was born in February 1942 in Monroe, Louisiana. Although he graduated from high school, Newton was functionally illiterate. Moving to California, Newton became involved in criminal activities as a pimp and armed robber and did time in prison. After his release, Newton taught himself to read, enrolling in Merritt College in 1966.

Bobby Seale was born in Dallas, Texas, in 1936 and served in the U.S. Air Force before moving to Oakland, California, to attend Merritt College. At Merritt College, Newton and Seale met the man who would become their mentor, Donald Warden.[162]

Warden led the college's Afro-American Association, known for its program on Bay Area radio station KDIA. Warden's commentary on the 1965 Watts riot was commemorated in a pressed vinyl recording called "Burn, Baby, Burn."[163] At Merritt, Newton and the other association members were exposed to anti-colonialist author Frantz Fanon (a Marxist and early critical race theorist and proponent of the Soviet-backed Algerian rebellion against France), Pan-African pro-Communist anti-colonialist leaders Kwame Nkrumah and Jomo

Kenyatta, and successful Communist guerrilla Mao Tse-Tung and the less successful Ernesto "Che" Guevara.[164]

Yet Newton's two largest influences were Robert F. Williams and the Lowndes County Freedom Organization, a project of the Students Non-Violent Coordinating Committee (SNCC), from which the name of the Black Panther Party would come.[165] It is worth examining both influences in some detail.

Robert F. Williams and the Revolutionary Action Movement (RAM)

Robert F. Williams grew up in Monroe, North Carolina, and, after a stint in Michigan as a union organizer for the United Auto Workers, returned to Monroe to participate in the civil rights movement as a chapter president of the NAACP. Williams's experience in North Carolina, which involved violent armed showdowns with the KKK, led him to adopt the view that the civil rights project could not be accomplished without armed self-defense. Williams founded the Black Armed Guard, a gun club chartered by the National Rifle Association, and began providing armed escorts for Freedom Riders.

Williams's early history was within the broader American tradition of Second Amendment rights and remains favorably cited today by gun rights supporters.[166] Yet by 1961, Williams was moving further to the left and associating with the Communist Party. He traveled to Cuba despite U.S. restrictions on travel and became a founding member of the Fair Play for Cuba Committee to support the Fidel Castro regime. Williams was known to fly a Cuban flag on his property and began issuing calls for armed revolution.[167]

Williams and his family eventually fled to Havana to avoid charges that he had kidnapped a white couple during a riot. While in Cuba in 1962, he published *Negroes with Guns*. The kidnapping case, described as "murky" in Williams' *New York Times* obituary, was eventually dropped in 1976.[168] *Negroes with Guns* became a central work for the

BPPSD, as former Panther Kathleen Cleaver explained:

> I saw it when I first came out to the Bay Area in July 1967, in Eldridge Cleaver's apartment. He had a whole case of them he was handing out. Anybody that came into the Black Panther Party had to get a copy of Negroes with Guns, they had to read it, and we had to discuss it.[169]

Williams also produced the Cuban-government-supported Radio Free Dixie program, where he promoted Cuban regime propaganda as well as his own vision for a black nationalist uprising initiated by urban guerrilla warfare, following the model being established in Latin America.[170] As can be seen from the Radio Free Dixie name, Williams's program perpetuated the Soviet effort of targeting America's "black belt" population throughout the deep South. Williams's flight to Cuba was likewise emulated by numerous Black Panther leaders in the years to follow.

In 1961, a number of black radical students left the Students for a Democratic Society to form the Revolutionary Action Movement (RAM). The organization was predominantly led by Donald Freeman and Maxwell Stanford, with guidance from Ethel Johnson, an organizer from Monroe, North Carolina, who worked closely with Williams. Through Johnson, the leaders of RAM were introduced to the work of black Communist Party organizers from the 1930s and 1940s, particularly Queen Mother Audley Moore, who became another mentor of the group. RAM was also heavily influenced by the rhetorical power of NOI's Malcolm X and counted NOI adherents who were loyal to Malcolm X as members. Both Newton and Seale participated with the Oakland chapter of RAM, which developed out of Warden's Afro-American Association at Merritt College.[171]

RAM's 12-point program included an above-ground Black Students organization, a "liberation" union of black workers, black rifle clubs to train a militia force, and an underground network of RAM cells to lead an urban guerrilla force. RAM doctrine emphasized the "development of the nation within a nation concept," echoing the earlier "black belt" language of the Comintern, arguing that black people represented "a captive nation suppressed and that their fight is not for integration into the white community but one of national liberation."[172]

By 1964, the group eventually met and coordinated with both Williams and Malcolm X, naming Williams its "international chairman" and Malcolm X its "international spokesman."[173]

The organization undertook an explicit effort to infiltrate the leading civil rights organizations of the period—including the SNCC, the Congress on Racial Equality, the NAACP, and Martin Luther King Jr.'s Southern Christian Leadership Conference—and to direct those groups to a more explicitly revolutionary, black liberation direction. It aggressively agitated for armed defense over non-violent demonstration.[174]

Following Malcolm X's split from NOI in 1965 and the formation of the OAAU, RAM viewed itself as the "paramilitary wing" of that organization.[175]

Newton and Seale's split from RAM is a matter of some dispute. Pro-RAM sources claim that Seale was expelled for drunkenness, while pro-BPPSD sources claim that RAM failed to follow through on its rhetoric when asked to adopt Newton's program of increasing confrontation with law enforcement.[176] While RAM remained active throughout the 1970s, including paying a pivotal role in the formation of the Republic of New Afrika, it lacked the massive cultural appeal of the BPPSD, and many of its adherents were subsumed into the Panther movement.

Stokely Carmichael and the Lowndes County Freedom Organization

The SNCC was originally founded as a student-led auxiliary of the SCLC formed in Nashville, Tennessee.[177] The organization quickly took on a prominent life of its own. The SNCC became one of the leading civil rights groups challenging Southern segregationist policies on interstate buses (which became known as "Freedom Riders") and eventually widened their scope to include other forms of segregation, with an emphasis on voter registration for blacks. Voter registration campaigns in Mississippi and southern Georgia stalled, however, due to resistance from state Democratic parties. This led the SNCC to see a need for creating full political parties, beginning with the Mississippi Freedom Democratic Party in April 1964.[178]

As part of its efforts, the SNCC zeroed in on Lowndes County, Alabama, which lay along the route of the famous march from Selma to Montgomery.[179] Lowndes featured the highest black population and the lowest black voter registration in the state and was known as "Bloody Lowndes" for its history of racial violence against blacks.[180]

To Lowndes came Trinidadian-born Stokely Carmichael. Raised in New York City and naturalized as a U.S. citizen, Carmichael attended the Bronx School of Science, where he became a close friend of Eugene Dennis Jr., whose father served as general secretary of the CPUSA,[181] and was introduced to many "black radicals and Communist activists."[182] The charismatic Carmichael joined the SNCC affiliate the Non-Violent Action Group at Howard University in 1960 and rose through the SNCC ranks to become SNCC chairman by 1966.

In Lowndes, Carmichael and the SNCC traded upon their affiliation with Martin Luther King Jr. and the SCLC to access the tight-knit rural community. Asked, "You one of Dr. King's men?" Carmichael reportedly replied, "Yes, Ma'am, I am."[183]

Yet for Carmichael, despite the SNCC's name, non-violence was not a guiding principle but merely a tactical consideration. As Carmichael himself explained in an interview from Havana, Cuba, in 1967:

> We used the name nonviolent because at that time Martin Luther King was the central figure of the black struggle and he was still preaching nonviolence, and anyone who talked about violence at that time was considered treasonable—amounting—to treason, so we decided that we would use the name nonviolent, but in the meantime we knew our struggle was not about to be nonviolent, but we would just wait until the time was right for the actual [word indistinct] name.

> We came together, we would coordinate activities between the students wherever we would have a nonviolent demonstration. But after 1 year many of us decided that demonstrations were not the answer.[184]

In Lowndes, carrying arms for self-defense became an increasingly common practice, as the SNCC and local volunteers worked to create the first all-black political party, the Lowndes County Freedom Organization (LCFO), which took as its symbol the black panther.[185] Protected by its armed members, the party was able to engage in mass meetings and political organizing activities despite intimidation.

With the successful passage of the 1965 Voting Rights Act and the arrival of federal voter registrars, the LCFO elected its first party members to county-wide office. The image of an all-black party under the banner of the black panther—successfully taking political control at the local level and backed by the carrying of arms—was a powerful one, and Black Panther parties came to emulate the LCFO throughout the country, including in Newton's Oakland.

Under Carmichael, the SNCC increasingly adopted a black separatist position under the slogan "Black Power." In 1966 the SNCC adopted as its formal position "The Basis for Black Power," which called for excluding whites from the organization and formally opposed integration in favor of separatism:

> These things which revolve around the right to organize have been accomplished mainly because of the entrance of white people into Mississippi, in the summer of 1964. Since these goals have now been accomplished, whites' role in the movement has now ended.... If we are to proceed toward true liberation, we must cut ourselves off from white people. We must form our own institutions, credit unions, co-ops, political parties, write our own histories.[186]

The SNCC's increasingly radical behavior culminated in violent riots around the country throughout the late 1960s, the most notable in Atlanta,[187] Nashville,[188] and Houston.[189] As the SNCC moved toward Black Power and away from American civil and equal rights, Carmichael made overtures toward Elijah Muhammad and NOI, praising the NOI leader publicly.[190]

Carmichael personally granted Newton the right to adopt the Black Panther name and image and in 1969 joined the BPPSD under the title "prime minister" before eventually breaking with the group to promote a Pan-African socialist agenda.[191]

Guns and Butter: The Black Panther Program

At the core of the BPPSD were Newton and Seale, soon joined by "Minister for Information" Eldridge Cleaver, a rapist, jail-house poet, and one time member of the NOI working as a writer for the New Left magazine *Ramparts* in Oakland while on parole.[192]

For public consumption, the 10-point program of the Black Panther Party cloaked itself in references to the U.S. Constitution and Declaration of Independence (as did many Communist and New Left groups), even while it contained obvious Marxist references such as "seizing the means of production" if the U.S. government refused to guarantee employment for all black men and proposing reparations for slavery.

The Black Panthers styled themselves as urban guerrilla fighters in accordance with the call from Robert F. Williams, who by 1966 was ensconced in Beijing as a guest of preeminent guerrilla warfare theorist and Chinese Communist dictator Mao Tse-Tung. Guerrilla warfare theory came to dominate Black Panther thinking.

While subsequent media coverage often portrays the Panthers' armed patrols and clashes with police as somehow incongruous with their free breakfast for children program, health clinics, and ambulance services, for the Panthers these efforts were merely two sides of the same guerrilla coin.[193] In 1967 Newton wrote "The Correct Handling of a Revolution" in which he discussed this dual focus:

> The primary job of the party is to provide leadership for the people. It must teach by words and action the correct strategic methods of prolonged resistance. When the people learn that it is no longer advantageous for them to resist by going into the streets in large numbers, and when they see the advantage in the activities of the guerrilla warfare method, they will quickly follow this example…. When the masses hear that a Gestapo policeman has been executed while sipping coffee at a counter, and the revolutionary executioners fled without being traced, the masses will see the validity of this kind of resistance. It is not necessary to organize thirty million Black people in primary groups of two's and three's, but it is important for the party to show the people how to stage a revolution…. The main purpose of the vanguard group should be to raise the consciousness of the masses through educational programs and other activities. The sleeping masses must be bombarded with the correct approach to struggle and the party must use all means available to get this information across to the masses.[194]

This type of activity became standard guerrilla warfare strategy worldwide, from Mao to Castro to Ho Chi Minh. In Vietnam it was known as "civic action" campaigns to support and induce compliance from civilian populations as integral parts of the insurgency, something the United States tried to mimic in its nation-building unconventional warfare approach for the next half-century or more. As Black Panther Party Chairman Fred Hampton put it in the 1969 essay "Power Anywhere Where There's People:"

> [T]hat's what the Breakfast for Children program is. A lot of people think it is charity, but what does it do? It takes the people from a stage to another stage. Any program that's revolutionary is an advancing program. Revolution is change. Honey, if you just keep on changing, before you know it, in fact, not even knowing what socialism is, you don't have to know what it is, they're endorsing it, they're participating in it, and they're supporting socialism.[195]

Newton's insistence on armed defense combined with aboveground programs was criticized by RAM, which likewise styled itself urban guerrillas but favored a wholly underground approach. For Newton the revolutionary act was necessarily public and performative, whether it was confronting police with armed force during traffic stops or hosting "liberation schools" in black neighborhoods.

No Panther act was more classically performative than the 1967 storming of the Sacramento Capitol building, where Panthers armed with shotguns and rifles entered the assembly building to protest the passage of the Mulford Act, a piece of gun control legislation aimed directly at the Panthers and their infamous open carrying of long guns.[196] The act passed in despite of, or perhaps because of, the Panther stunt. Newton, Seale, and other Panthers faced criminal charges.[197]

The Black Panther leadership constantly reminded its cadres of their guerrilla focus. Each prospective Panther was provided with a copy of Mao's "3 Main Rules of Discipline and 8 Points for Attention," a memorandum for the People's Liberation Army on how a guerrilla force should interact with civilians, including some instructions incongruous with the Black Panthers' urban environs such as "don't damage crops."[198]

Despite instructions such as ""don't take a single needle or piece of thread from the masses" and prohibitions against the possession or use of narcotics, the BPPSD sought out membership among street criminals and gang members, who were seen as the most genuinely and naturally revolutionary group.[199] As Eldridge Cleaver elaborated in his 1969 essay "On Ideology:"

> O.K. We are Lumpen. Right on. The Lumpenproletariat are all those who have no secure relationship or vested interest in the means of production and the institutions of capitalist society.... Also the so-called "Criminal Element," those who live by their wits, existing off that which they rip off, who stick guns in the faces of businessmen and say "stick 'em up," or "give it up"! Those who don't even want a job, who hate to work and can't relate to punching some pig's time clock, who would rather punch a pig in the mouth and rob him than punch that same pig's time clock and work for him, those whom Huey P. Newton calls "the illegitimate capitalists." In short, all those who simply have been locked out of the economy and robbed of their rightful social heritage.[200]

In a traditional Marxist context, the lumpenproletariat represents the undesirable and often criminal element of the working class that lacked class consciousness and was a potential weapon of the bourgeois class. While some Maoist theory acknowledged that the lumpenproleriat might have revolutionary possibility, it was Frantz Fanon in *Wretched of the Earth* (1961) who popularized the term for a new American audience and led to its being adopted by the Black Panthers, as Cleaver notes in his essay.

Newton and Cleaver's emphasis on the so-called criminal element didn't necessarily engender good discipline, even if their provocative stances were good for recruitment. As former Black Panther field marshal Donald Cox noted:

> We started organizing, trying to get as many Blacks together as possible. Getting guns; it wasn't a real

well-disciplined organization at the time, cause some people started doing all kinds of crazy stuff, cheap, nickel & dime robberies, intimidating people & whatnot, but still it was growing like wildfire.[201]

These aggressive public displays of open defiance enamored new members, and the BPPSD soon spread coast to coast. But these behaviors also drew police attention, and conflicts with law enforcement eventually claimed the lives of both police officers and Panthers alike. By 1969 approximately 30 Panthers had been killed, nearly all of them in shootouts with police or in confrontations with rival black militants.[202]

Following Newton's 1967 arrest for the murder of Oakland police officer John Frey during a traffic stop, Eldridge Cleaver took increasing leadership of the organization and interjected a more offensive mode into the BPPSD. As Burrough writes in *Days of Rage*:

> Newton and Seale were using "armed self-defense" as a recruiting tool, a way to lure members to man the education, welfare, and free-breakfast programs the Panthers were putting into place; for all their tough talk, they had no intention of actually hunting policemen. Cleaver did. He wanted the bloody fight Malcolm [X] and [SNCC leader] H. Rap Brown foresaw; a genuine revolution, Vietnam-style guerrilla warfare in America. Many found this hard to take seriously, but Cleaver was serious.[203]

Two days after the assassination of Martin Luther King Jr. on April 4, 1968, amid the subsequent rioting, Cleaver and other Panthers, including 18-year-old Panther Bobby Hutton, acted on the rhetoric and went out hunting. For many years the Panthers and their New Left allies claimed that Oakland police stopped Cleaver and Hutton, but as Cleaver later admitted, the police were deliberately ambushed.[204]

During the shootout that followed, Hutton was killed, becoming the quintessential Panther martyr. Cleaver was charged with attempted murder and jumped bail, fleeing first to Cuba and then Algeria, where he ensconced himself as the head of the Panthers' "International Section." He was soon joined by a small coterie of other wanted Panthers.[205]

Newton Reasserts Control

With both Newton and Cleaver facing murder charges, the day-to-day operation of the Panthers fell largely to Bobby Seale and Chief of Staff David Hillard, who, known for keeping a photograph of Josef Stalin in his office, exhibited an increasingly paranoid streak and attempted to establish stricter centralization on the rapidly growing organization. Former Panther field marshal Donald Cox wrote:

> Adopting the Marxist Leninist structure of the party, with democratic centralism as its soul, all power was then confiscated in the name of the central committee, which, in reality, meant just David Hilliard, the party's chief of staff, and Bobby Seale, the party's cofounder. In name I was a member of the central committee from the time I met Bobby at the beginning of 1968 until I resigned in the autumn of 1973, and during that time there was never one meeting of the central committee, nor were there ever points at which members of the central committee were asked to vote on any proposition. Or, if there was, I was never told about it. Whenever David or Bobby thought up anything, it was simply sent down through the organization as a directive from the central committee.[206]

The Panthers' newspaper regularly included sections listing the names of Panthers purged from the rolls during this internal house cleaning. These were the lucky ones. Illiterate 18-year-old Panther recruit Alex Rackley was interrogated, tortured, and murdered on suspicion of being a police informant.[207] Panther member Warren Kimbro later testified that the murder "was a party function, and an order" as well as "a part of the purge."[208] Seale faced conspiracy charges for ordering the killing but was not convicted.[209] Rumors of a Panther killing ground in the mountains of Santa Cruz were rampant among New Left figures,[210] and at least one body—that of Panther Fred Bennett—was found near the site of an apparent bomb factory containing sticks of dynamite, blasting camps, timers, and other equipment.[211]

With Newton released on appeal in 1971, he began to reassert himself over the organization, and differences in approach between himself and Cleaver became increasingly impossible to paper over. While Cleaver in Algeria sought an offensive strategy, desiring to build an underground army to target police across the country, Newton was increasingly focused on the group's community programs, which were lavishly funded by pro-Panther groupies among California's well-to-do.

In 1971, Newton expelled Cleaver from the BPPSD. In describing what he called Cleaver's "defection," Newton wrote:

> Under the influence of Eldridge Cleaver, the Party gave the community no alternative for dealing with us, except by picking up the gun. This move was reactionary simply because the community was not at that point. Instead of being a cultural cult group, we became, by that act, a revolutionary cult group. But this is a basic contradiction, because revolution is a process, and if the acts you commit do not fall within the scope of the process then they are non-revolutionary. What the revolutionary movement and the Black community needs is a very strong structure. This structure can only exist with the support of the

> people and it can only get its support through serving them. This is why we have the service to the people program—the most important thing in the Party. We will serve their needs, so that they can survive through this oppression. Then when they are ready to pick up the gun, serious business will happen.[212]

For Newton, Cleaver's approach was too similar to the RAM approach he had criticized several years earlier: too underground, without enough work to ingratiate the Panthers into the black community at large.

And while the stated ideological goal for Newton was to "put away the gun" and build "survival programs" for the black community, in practice these projects became both funding and cover for a criminal enterprise, which included extorting local black-owned liquor stores and strong-arming pimps and drug dealers.[213] Former New Left leaders Peter Collier and David Horowitz wrote that "even while launching the school and survival programs, in other words, Huey was conceiving a parallel strategy to take over the vice in Oakland."[214]

This intimidation extended both inside the BPPSD and to the community at large, as Berkeley journalist Kate Coleman, known for her exposé of the Panthers, wrote:

> The party in Oakland operated a virtual vice ring out of Newton's favorite nighttime haunt, the Lamp Post bar. From its smoky recesses, the Panthers under Newton conducted a reign of terror, punishing rank-and-file females for even minor "infractions" by turning them out as prostitutes. Newton led an extortion racket against Oakland's bars, nightclubs, pimps and dope dealers, and his handpicked squad of collectors turned nasty whenever anyone failed to pay protection money. The Fox-Oakland theater was torched two times in 1973, its owner told me, after the owner refused to

hire a quota of Panthers and to pay for protection.²¹⁵

Newton was accused of murdering a prostitute and fled to Cuba in 1974. He eventually returned to the United States and was acquitted after "a planned assassination" attempt of the "most important witness" in the case.²¹⁶

Newton's downward spiral into street crime continued, unchecked, until his death in 1989 at the hands of a drug dealer and member of the black supremacist prison gang the Black Guerrilla Family (BGF).²¹⁷ Ironically, the BGF was founded by prison radical, gangster, and author George Jackson, who was himself a Panther field marshal. The Panthers played a role in the 1971 escape attempt that led to Jackson's death and "martyrdom" at the hands of prison guards.²¹⁸

Black Panthers

>Founder: Huey P. Newton
>Established: 1966 in Oakland, California
>Notable Members: Stokely Carmichael, Bobby Seale, Eldridge Cleaver
>Summary of Ideology: armed black liberation through Marxist-Maoist guerrilla warfare principles with post-colonial influences from Frantz Fanon and others
>Subgroups/Affiliated Groups: Black Liberation Army
>Estimated Adherents: 5,000-10,000 members
>Distinguishing Practices: uniform of black berets and leather jackets, carrying of long guns, emphasis on public armed demonstrations

CHAPTER FOUR
BLACK LIBERATION ARMY

While Newton returned from prison to reestablish control over the cash cow that was the Panthers' various community programs, Eldridge Cleaver was in Algiers, popularized by Fanon and then known as the "liberation capital of the Third World." Led by the National Liberation Front (FLN), former guerrillas turned Algerian government, Algiers at the time had an almost Wild West, Casbalanca-esque vibe, filled as it was various foreign "embassies" of Soviet-backed guerrillas and national liberation organizations ranging from the Palestine Liberation Organization to the African National Congress.[219]

Algeria made sense as an international getaway for Cleaver and the Panthers. Panther-friendly Cuba was among the first to recognize the Algerian revolutionary government, and Algeria made a useful base for Cuban forays into both Africa and the Middle East. Ernesto "Che" Guevera had established close ties with Algeria's first president, Ben Bella, and in 1965 made Algiers the home of Cuba's African Liberation Committee, from which he launched a failed expedition into Congo.[220]

While Cleaver initially denied that the Black Panthers/BLA received training and aid from Communist Cuba, Jaime Suchlicki of the Cuban Studies Institute has argued that Cuba did play a role in providing weapons and explosives training to the Panthers both via Cuban agents in Canada and during the Panthers' time in Havana.[221]

In Algiers, Cleaver was surrounded with genuine—and genuinely violent—revolutionaries and terrorists and enjoyed a government stipend to be a professional revolutionary. He was situated in a well-appointed guest house amid a collection of AK-47s, including one gifted to him by North Korean dictator Kim Il-Sung, which he later allegedly used to murder fellow Panther Clinton Rahim Smith.[222]

Expelled from the Panthers by Newton, Cleaver launched the Revolutionary People's Communication Network (RCPN)—described as "not an organization but a network of communication and coordination link-ups between various worldwide organizations of struggle"—with the help of wife Kathleen Cleaver, who was able to travel back and forth to the United States, along with a handful of other Panthers.[223] The RCPN launched a magazine to mirror the one he had edited for the Panthers, which became known as *Babylon*, a nickname used to describe the United States.

Formation and Ideology

The RCPN was just a front for what Cleaver really had in mind: a genuine black guerrilla network along the lines of the Algerian FLN, which he understood to consist primarily of four elements: (1) a small political control group responsible for political messaging, (2) publication of the newspaper and administrative tasks, (3) a prisoner support network, and (4) a "liaison" section of white allies who provided logistical and other support. Perhaps most importantly, the military section, compromised of three-man cells of "commandos" who were isolated from other cells and from the political section but were vertically integrated into the organization as a whole. This guerrilla force was likewise divided between a rural (mostly Southern) black homeland (along the lines of the Soviet "black belt" thesis) and the urban areas, which were compared to France versus Algeria proper:

> In the incipient stages of armed revolutionary struggle, in Babylon, the beginnings of a similar separation of functions, united at the top, can already be seen developing. The situation of the black community in the large urban centers of Babylon can be roughly

> compared to that of Algerians in France at the time of the war of national liberation: a large, active minority of disenfranchised citizens, unemployed and underemployed, exploited, victimized and brutalized on the basis of race, culturally alienated within the mother country, and without a land base. The comparison can be pushed even further, though obviously not to its limits, if we can think of the large black rural population of Amerikkka as comparable to that of Algeria proper: disinherited peasants, landless agricultural workers, rural stagnation, and rural exodus. The heart of revolutionary struggle lay in this Algeria where a guerrilla army of peasants and the jobless were engaged in revolutionary warfare.[224]

The goal of this structure was to keep the military units capable of independent action and allow an above-ground support structure to develop without being immediately overwhelmed by the police, as the Panthers had been, nor to be without an above-ground presence, as RAM had been.

That group of armed cells would come to be called the Black Liberation Army (BLA). While Cleaver had originally preferred the name Afro-American Liberation Army (AALA), the BLA stuck, in part probably because the name was foreshadowed in prior Panther publications. The Panther Rules explicitly prohibited Panthers from joining any military formation other than the previously entirely theoretical BLA.[225]

In practice, these autonomous action cells found it difficult to coordinate with Cleaver and the upper leadership, as BLA member Blood McCreary explained to Bryan Burrough in *Days of Rage*:

> I never understood the concept of an organization without leadership. I always thought that was going to

be difficult and it was. When we got into the field, we were supposed to be autonomous, and you'd be two or three cells trying to do their own thing. I remember once two cells showed up to rob the same bank.[226]

The autonomous structure helped to undermine police investigation, however, as law enforcement initially rejected the notion that the BLA was a real conspiracy rather than merely a fanciful name, just an idea for a series of independent extremists. As an NYPD press release described:

> Intelligence fails to identify a formal structure of a firm organization known as the Black Liberation Army. It is more likely that various extremist individuals, 75 to 100 in number, are making use of the name Black Liberation Army in order to give some semblance of legitimacy to these homicidal acts. These individuals form and dissolve and reform in small groups or cells.[227]

While the BLA was challenging to manage, its goal was to avoid repeating mistakes made by the Panthers, as an anonymous BLA manual entitled *The Revolutionary Armed Struggle* explained under the heading "Lessons from Tactical Errors." Such errors included mixing political activists and "military combatants" within the same households, the open display of weapons for non-operational purposes, and the fighting of pitched battles over buildings or property, all of which had been common behavior for the Black Panthers.[228] The document also contained what can be read as a critique of Newton and an explanation for Cleaver's next move:

> If a revolutionary leader should decide to abrogate the original objective solely because of the State's opposition, this is likely to be liberalism or revisionism, and he or she will be subverting the movement, and

destroying the militancy of the masses.

At this time it would be best for leaders to direct a part or the whole organization to begin functioning clandestinely (underground); while a part relinquishes offensive resistance and establishes a purely legal political posture or a new (aboveground) organization in place of the one that has gone underground. In this way, the momentum of the struggle continues, the political objective is not compromised, while an active clandestine organization preserves the militancy and defense of the political mass movement.

This dual approach of an armed clandestine underground and an unarmed overt political wing ultimately featured among Soviet-backed insurgencies worldwide.

With Cleaver deliberately isolating himself from the tactical side, actual leadership of the BLA fell to Donald Cox as Cleaver's military advisor and Nathaniel Burns, aka Sekou Odinga, together with a handful of Panthers in New York, including Dhoruba Moore and his longtime friends Zayd and Lumumba Shakur.[229] Indeed, the entirety of the BLA was mostly represented by New York City–based Panthers, the only Panther chapter that refused to come under Newton's thumb when the Black Panther founder resumed command.

The New York Panthers had always been a step removed from the Oakland-based Panther Party's dominating influence. According to Maxwell Stanford of RAM, the New York Black Panthers were originally founded separately from the Oakland Panthers out of a coalition of SNCC and RAM members.[230] The New York members were far more steeped in the teachings of Malcolm X, far more Pan-African in their outlook, favoring dashikis over black berets and leather and taking African names—all behaviors disapproved of by Oakland. They were also more aggressive, confrontational, and infatuated with the notion of working underground.[231] The decision to side with Cleaver makes sense, given he had formerly worked with Malcolm X's OAAU, and his wife Kathleen was a New York, not a West Coast, Panther and was Cleaver's main link back to America.[232]

But separated by distance and by practicalities of BLA's vision of autonomous warfare, the BLA, once it began its bloody campaign on May 19, 1971 (the birthdays of Malcolm X and Ho Chi Minh), until its death knell in the early years of the 1980s, the various BLA cadres were ultimately on their own for support.

BLA and Carlos Marighela

The BLA took as its operating manual a work by Brazilian Communist and theorist of urban guerrilla warfare Carlos Marighela called the *Minimanual of the Urban Guerrilla*. BLA leader Donald Cox cited Marighela frequently in his own guerrilla writings.[233] As Marighela wrote, the two primary focuses for the urban guerrilla were:

> a) the physical liquidation of the chiefs and assistants of the armed forces and of the police;
>
> b) the expropriation of government resources and those belonging to the big capitalists ... with small expropriations used for the maintenance of individual urban guerrillas and large ones for the sustenance of the revolution itself.[234]

For Marighela, and for BLA fighters, these acts of robbery and murder were themselves political acts to undermine the government as a whole while sustaining the urban guerrilla. As an FBI law enforcement bulletin from 1974 explains:

> Marighela's overall theory of revolution differed from that of orthodox Marxists. Instead of an uprising by

politically indoctrinated masses led by an indigenous communist party the urban guerrilla's theory of revolution is to demonstrate that the government is incapable of fulfilling its primary purpose, that of providing a stable, ordered society. If this basic function of government is eroded in practice, then the masses will reject the government in power. Rejection will come about through revolution, which will come to fruition when the most visible symbol of government, law enforcement, is shown to be impotent in battling the guerrilla. Hence, the primary objective of attacking police officer; If the police cannot protect themselves, how can they protect the citizenry—their basic function?[235]

For Marighela, it was also vital that such attacks were accompanied by declarations or manifestos. Only by sharing the political nature of the crime could the violence be justified as a revolutionary attack. As Marighela instructs in the *Minimanual*:

> A consistent propaganda by letters sent to specific addresses, explaining the meaning of the urban guerrilla's armed actions, produces considerable results and is one method of influencing certain segments of the population.[236]

Marighela has recently reemerged in the public consciousness—and even a level of mainstream popularity—following a 2019 biopic directed by Wagner Moura, one of the lead actors from the hit Netflix TV show *Narcos*.[237]

The BLA upheld the principle of armed propaganda as Marighela instructed, mailing typewritten letters and shell casings to the *New York Times* and other New York media following its first police assassination explaining its purpose:

> Revolutionary justice has been meted out again by righteous brothers of the Black Liberation Army with the death of two Gestapo pigs gunned down as so many of our brothers have been gunned down in the past. But this time no racist class jury acquite [*sic*] them. Revolutionary Justice is ours!²³⁸

Assata: "Unreconstructed Insurrectionist"

Perhaps the most well-known member of the BLA is Joanne Chesimard (*nom de guerre* Assata Shakur), who remains on the FBI's Most Wanted Terrorist list for the murder of New Jersey state trooper Werner Foerster in 1973. Still a fugitive in Cuba, Assata Shakur is the closest female analogue to the ubiquitous Che Guevara, with t-shirts and posters often featuring her "inspirational" quotes and poetry.

Shakur's work, principally her memoir written in Cuba, has been lionized and used as a teaching text in certain university settings. As one writer describes:

> First published in 1987, and reissued in 2001, lots of people have started to study this book again, drawn by the allure of Assata's revolutionary life, which began with her association with the Black Panther Party in the late 1960s.... The memoir remains an invaluable record of Assata as a teacher-organizer; she shares how she became a student, a community educator, and an "unreconstructed insurrectionist," in the words of the movement scholar Joy James. Using narrative and poetry to tell her own story, Assata implicitly models how readers can commit their own lives to social change.²³⁹

Historically, however, it is far from clear that Shakur played a significant ideological or intellectual role within the BLA. Burrough argues in *Days of Rage* that Shakur's popularity was in part a consequence of the fixation by New York police. As one investigator put it, "Was she the heart and soul of the BLA? Hell, no.... [W]e created that myth, the cops did."[240]

Yet Assata Shakur remains an icon for imitation among modern-day black liberation organizations. Black Lives Matter co-founder Alicia Garza described her devotion: "When I use Assata's powerful demand in my organizing work, I always begin by sharing where it comes from, sharing about Assata's significance to the Black Liberation Movement, what it's [sic] political purpose and message is, and why it's important in our context."[241]

One phrase in particular came to be called "Assata's chant," cribbed partially from the *Communist Manifesto*, during the 2020 George Floyd uprising because it was so pervasive: "It is our duty to fight for our freedom. It is our duty to win. We must love each other and support each other. We have nothing to lose but our chains."[242] It was even mainstreamed as an introduction to an NAACP conference in 2019 that was attended by many notable Democratic Party leaders and led to statement of condemnation from New Jersey state officials who pointed out Shakur's role in the murder of a police officer.[243]

Unlike Shakur, most other BLA members were either killed in gun battles with police or faced long prison sentences, many of which have only recently come to an end. Even from behind prison bars, several BLA figures went on to advance a black liberation ideology for the 21st century.

For his part, Eldridge Cleaver eventually returned to the United States, renounced his previous associations, and became a born-again Christian. He eventually adopted an anti-communist message as a Republican political figure before succumbing to drug abuse and health problems in his later years.[244]

Black Liberation Army

Founder: Eldridge Cleaver
Established: 1965 in Algiers
Notable Members: Donald Cox, Kathleen Cleaver, Assata Shakur, Sekou Odinga, Dhoruba Moore, Zayd Shakur, Lumumba Shakur
Summary of Ideology: armed revolution against the United States through an autonomous cellular network of urban guerrillas targeting police to undermine order
Subgroups/Affiliated Groups: Black Panther Party
Distinguishing Practices: autonomous structure, distribution of communiques, targeted killing of police, armed robberies

CHAPTER FIVE:
INTERACTIONS WITH LAW ENFORCEMENT

Cop-Watching and Armed Demonstrations

The Black Panther Party was the first group to practice and popularize the technique now known as "cop-watching." Cop-watching is defined as a form of "community self-defense" where participants deliberately surveil police officers in the performance of their duties and may seek to intervene or interject when law enforcement is interacting with a member of the public.[245] They are often explicitly organized around anti-capitalist and anti-police slogans[246] and presume that law enforcement deliberately and routinely violates the rights and engage in violence against racial and other minorities.[247] Cop-watching has proliferated in the past two decades, an outcome attributed to both the prevalence of smartphone technology and a number of high-profile incidents.[248]

Burrough describes the earliest Black Panther efforts:

> [The Black Panthers] began their patrols, cruising the streets until they found a black citizen being questioned by the police, typically at a traffic stop. The Panthers would step from their car, guns drawn, and remind the citizen of his rights; when a shaken patrolmen asked what the hell they were doing. Newton, who had taken law school classes, told him of their right to bear arms.[249]

Unlike the Panthers, modern cop-watchers are typically unarmed, with some exceptions.[250] One current example of an armed BIE group that does promote cop-watching is the Huey P. Newton Gun Club (HPN-GC) based in Dallas, Texas. The group's website notes:

> We, the Huey P Newton Gun Club, mobilize and organize for an end to police brutality and misconduct. We demand the police in our community, and elsewhere, respect the Human Rights of our people and their constitutional rights. We strive for community police review boards with legal power to seek indictments, punish and discipline rogue police officers. *We will monitor and observe the police according to the law.*[251]

While the group stresses that it is not a reincarnation of the Black Panthers, among its "Alpha Company requirements and guidelines" is the demand that members "Respect ALL elders and former members of the BPP, BLA, SNCC, PG-RNA [Provisional Government-Republic of New Afrika], and RAM."[252]

Whether cop-watchers are armed or not, police leaders have expressed concerns that cop-watching can be dangerous to law enforcement, as it often results in distracting officers and escalating tensions during already tense moments, such as during traffic stops. Former NYPD Commissioner William Bratton noted, "There is increasing efforts on the part of individuals—sometimes in a crowd and oftentimes mobs—to attempt to record, intimidate and create fear and physically free a prisoner."[253]

Related to cop-watching is the practice of providing armed defense of protests and demonstrations, another example of Newton's high-profile but ostensibly legal tactics. The modern proliferation of armed demonstrations and providing security escorts for marches and protests is by no means limited to BIE groups and now appears among political protests across the spectrum, but it is fair to say that it was largely pioneered by the Black Panthers, who popularized armed defense. The Panthers' 1967 effort to provide "security" for Malcolm X's widow Betty Shabazz is a case in point.

81

Shabazz was making a high-profile visit to the offices of the New Left magazine *Ramparts*. The Oakland Panthers provided an armed security force for Shabazz, who was already surrounded by journalists and law enforcement officers. When a photographer refused to obey Newton's commands, he was assaulted. The Black Panthers then used their firearms to force police to deescalate, achieving a propaganda victory.[254]

Armed defense can play a similar role in modern protests. While organizers may claim that firearms are present only to defend protestors from expected violence from counter-protestors, in fact the presence of firearms by BIE is often calculated to intimidate law enforcement and may force officers to tolerate violations of the law they might otherwise enforce. As one practitioner describes:

> As the Black Militant Liberation group the Black Panthers showed back in the 1960s, as the [Mexican] Zapatistas showed in the '90s, and as anarchists in New Orleans showed during the aftermath of Katrina, when cops and other fascists see that they're not the only one's packing, the balance of power shifts, and they tend to reconsider their tactics.[255]

BIE groups will often openly express that their arms are intended to counter police "repression" or "police terrorism," and—similar to the progression of Robert F. Williams—they are intended to eventually foster an armed resistance. Erick Khafre, founder of the HPN-GC, says:

> I envision that the HPN-GC will be a spark for armed resistance and self defense throughout the country. It is my hope that we can pass our courage and skills on to the youth to prepare them to take community defense to a new level.[256]

Like the Panthers before them, the carrying of weapons is seen not within the context of traditional American rights as individuals but rather as part of a communal and racial separatist effort. Indeed, a local Texas Second Amendment group attempted to cooperate with the Dallas-based HPN-GC to highlight the importance of gun rights, only to be aggressively rebuffed.[257]

HPN-GC co-founder Kilaika Anayejali Kwa Baruti says:

> Armed self-defense is a necessity when it comes to self-determination. When we as African people create and build institutions, gain control of our own resources, and determine our own destinies in every respect, we must be able to defend and secure what we create.[258]

Obviously, the presence of significant numbers of armed protestors increases the probability of an incident, even unintentionally. In one example, a member of the black militia NFAC (Not F**cking Around Coalition) had a negligent discharge, wounding herself and two other members of the group. The leader of that organization, who goes by the name GrandMaster Jay and who had instructed his followers to "burn government officials' homes and murder their children" on social media, was indicted by DOJ after pointing a rifle at federal agents observing an armed march from atop a nearby building in 2020.[259]

Ultimately, the bearing of arms during a political demonstration in a manner consistent with state and local law is protected under the First and Second amendments, irrespective of the political content of that demonstration. Still, law enforcement should be aware of the reality that demonstrations by armed BIEs, whose ideology proposes the overthrow of the U.S. Constitution in the form of carving out a separatist black state or establishing a revolutionary communist state, generates a different threat profile from demonstrations organized around a traditional public support for enumerated constitutional rights.

In some cases, the carrying of firearms in public display may give BIEs confidence to move forward with more aggressive plans in the same way that the BPPSD's armed facing off against police ultimately inspired Cleaver to launch the BLA.

Targeting of Police Officers: Traffic Stops

The rise of the Black Power movement, refined by the Panthers and escalating with the formation of the BLA, paralleled an exponential rise in the levels of violence against police. Attacks on police officers rose meteorically from 1964 to 1969, much of which authorities attributed to the Panthers. As Burrough writes, "Between 1964 and 1969 assaults on Los Angeles patrolmen quintupled. Between 1967 and 1969 attacks on officers in New Jersey leaped by 41 percent. In Detroit they rose 70 percent in 1969 alone."[260] The Black Panthers and the spin-off BLA killed at least 15 police officers during their relative short period of operation.[261] Other sources put the number killed by the BLA alone at 20,[262] and others have put the total closer to 35.[263] Despite being responsible for a remarkably high number of murders in a relatively short period, there is very little available online about these attacks, while most articles detail stories of Black Panthers killed by police.

Much of the Panther violence against police fell into one of two categories: interactions at traffic stops that devolved into shoot-outs and the deliberate targeting of police for assassination, usually in the form of ambushes. In some cases, such as that of Eldridge Cleaver's gunfight with police, the press presented a deliberate ambush of police as the result of a traffic altercation.

Traffic stops were particularly fraught because the Panthers routinely travelled with long guns as part of their community patrolling efforts, and the group's rhetoric had adherents convinced that the police were set on deliberately murdering Panthers. Meanwhile, Panther propaganda convinced law enforcement (with good reason) that Panthers were prepared to murder police. As a result, encounters were volatile and easily degenerated into violence.

On October 28, 1967, Newton was pulled over in a traffic stop by two Oakland police officers, John Frey and Herbert Heanes. The car Newton was driving had multiple warrants associated with it.[264] An altercation ensued, and Frey was shot and killed and Heanes wounded. Newton himself sustained a bullet wound to the abdomen. The prosecution argued that Newton murdered Frey, while the defense claimed Frey was killed by friendly fire from one of the responding officers. Newton was convicted, but the verdict was overturned on appeal.[265] The circus of a trial and related "Free Huey!" campaign catapulted the Panthers to national renown and significantly expanded the group's recruiting. Newton later admitted to a fellow Panther that he had in fact killed Frey, yet it remains an article of faith among many that Newton's arrest was an example of police abuse.[266]

Some incidents were not necessarily ideological but resulted from officers interrupting felonious activities in progress. Such was the case of Officers Thomas Johnson and Charles Thomasson of the Nashville Police Department. On January 16, 1968, the officers spotted a vehicle that was wanted in connection with passing fake money orders. According to radio communications from that night, Officer Thomasson spotted the vehicle and attempted to make a traffic stop. The driver, Steven Parker, then attempted to run over Thomasson and fled. Thomasson pursued, joined by Officer Johnson. They followed the vehicle into a dead-end street, where three of the suspects jumped out, armed with long guns including a .30-30 rifle, and opened fire, killing both officers. Inside the vehicle, investigators found stolen money orders and stamps for processing them as well as Black Panther literature. Ralph Canady, Steven Parker, William Garvin Allen, Charles Lee Herron, and Charles Alexander were all convicted.[267]

A significant number of the BLA's murders of police officers took place during traffic stops, the most famous being Assata Shakur and her BLA cell murdering New Jersey State Trooper Werner Foerster. While primarily based in New York City, the BLA had established a training camp in the outskirts of Atlanta and ranged up and down the East Coast and Midwest seeking safe houses and planning and conducting bank robberies in order to raise funds for their guerrilla war.[268] As a result, unsuspecting police officers on traffic stops repeatedly found themselves facing heavily armed urban guerrillas prepared to unleash almost immediate murderous force upon being stopped. As one BLA member noted, "Our younger guys.... If a cop stopped us, they always wanted to shoot."[269]

On November 11, 1971, Lieutenant Ted Elmore of the Catawba Sheriff's Office was shot and paralyzed by multiple BLA members while conducting a routine stop. BLA members Robert Brown, William Owens, Avon White, and Fred Hilton were in one vehicle traveling from a Chattanooga, Tennessee, safehouse back to New York City to begin their operations. The Officer Down Memorial Page describes the assault:

> Unbeknownst to Lieutenant Elmore, he had stopped two members of the radical Black Panthers who had shot and wounded an Atlanta, Georgia, police officer several weeks earlier. As he exited his patrol car the occupants of the vehicle opened fire, striking him in the right arm, disabling it. As he tried to draw his weapon with his left hand he was shot again in the abdomen and fell to the ground. The assailants then shot him a third time, hitting him in the back, severing his spinal cord and causing paralysis. The suspects abandoned their car and fled into a nearby wooded area. After a massive manhunt both [White and Hilton] were apprehended. Their car was found to contain several rifles, three shotguns, a bazooka, and 14,000 rounds of ammunition.[270]

White and Hilton were later caught at a roadblock and charged with carrying concealed weapons, while Brown and Owens were convicted of assault.[271] Elmore suffered in paralysis for more than a decade, eventually dying of wounds from the attack.

It was another traffic stop shootout that finally cracked the case on the BLA and made it impossible for law enforcement to ignore that a genuine urban guerrilla operation was taking place. That was the St. Louis, Missouri, shootout between BLA members Blood McCreary, Ronald Carter, Tywon Meyers, and Henry "Sha Sha" Brown and local police.

Part of the Assata Shakur–Ronald Carter BLA Cell, which had just conducted a Miami bank robbery, the four BLA members traveled to St. Louis to establish yet another safe house when a sharp-eyed St. Louis police officer noticed a temporary Michigan license plate on the vehicle and pulled it over. During the stop, the officer noticed the vehicle was registered in Florida and that driver McCreary presented a counterfeit license from North Carolina. The officer ordered the occupants out of the car, at which time passengers in the rear seat opened fire, striking the officer in the stomach and legs. The BLA vehicle fled but was pursued, eventually crashing into a chain-link fence, where the BLA members continued to exchange rounds with police.

When the smoke cleared, Carter was dead, hit by one of his comrade's bullets. Brown and McCreary were captured, and Meyers escaped. Inside the car were more than a dozen guns, including rifles. "If we could have gotten to the M16 or the .30-06 we would've gotten away," McCreary noted.[272] One of the firearms found at the scene was the duty weapon of NYPD officer Rocco Laurie, whom the BLA had assassinated two weeks earlier.

While officer tactics for dealing with traffic stops have developed substantially since the 1970s, the stops remain one of the most dangerous of law enforcement's many duties. According to *Making It Safer: A Study of Law Enforcement Fatalities Between 2010-2016*, a report sponsored by the Office of Community Oriented Policing Services:

> Traffic Stops continued to be the most common self-initiated incident that led to officer fatalities,

accounting for 38, or 52 percent, of all 73 Self-Initiated Activity cases examined. The public encounters law enforcement officers most often during these stops for traffic violations; therefore, it makes sense that these stops are the independent enforcement action with the highest number of law enforcement fatalities.[273]

So while traffic stops remain dangerous for police, efforts to propagandize traffic stops as being especially racist and dangerous for black citizens increased in the wake of the death of Michael Brown in Ferguson, Missouri, and the subsequent rioting in 2014. In a politicized DOJ report, the Obama Administration insisted that the Ferguson police department was institutionally racist in the manner it conducted traffic stops despite the fact that "the numbers actually suggest that Ferguson police may be slightly less likely to pull over black drivers than are their national counterparts."[274]

A nationwide campaign in 2023 sought to eliminate police officers' ability to make traffic stops for a variety of violations under the claim that stops are mere "pretexts" based on racial animus.[275] Police-initiated interactions by traffic stop do appear to be dropping off slightly as of this writing. From 2015 to 2020, police-initiated contacts with civilians via traffic stop reduced from 11 percent (either driver or passenger contact) to 9 percent.[276] There is also some indication that traffic stops between police and black citizens have become more acrimonious, as the number of black citizens reporting that they received threats of force or non-lethal use of force from officers increased slightly from 3.8 percent in 2018 to 4.3 percent in 2020.

Targeting of Police Officers: Ambushes

Perhaps even more dangerous to law enforcement has been the significant increase in premeditated ambush attacks against police. Studies suggest that increases in ambush attacks since 2016 have been dramatic. From 2020 to 2021 ambushes against police increased 139 percent, and ambushes were already up 90 percent in 2020 over preceding years.[277]

Chief Joel F. Shults, writing for the National Police Association, notes that ambushes against police tend to take one of two forms: either "entrapment" or "spontaneous."

> Entrapment ambushes are planned by the perpetrator to lure officers into a surprise attack. Spontaneous ambushes are crimes of opportunity where a person has a predisposition and the means to attack a police officer who has the misfortune of encountering a killer with no warning.[278]

The BLA pioneered both types of ambushes in the United States. The killings of officers Waverly Jones and Joseph Piagentini are among the best example of the "entrapment" style. Jones and Piagentini were working the 32nd NYPD precinct, which included numerous public housing and private apartment complexes. The officers received a call regarding a domestic disturbance involving a woman who had been stabbed. When they arrived, however, the woman denied needing police assistance, and the two officers departed the scene. As they made their way back to their patrol car, Black Panthers Anthony Bottom (aka Jalil Abdul Muntaqim), Albert "Nuh" Washington, and Herman Bell ambushed them from behind.

Burrough describes the attack:

> Officer Jones, who was black, was struck three times, first in the back of the head, then twice in the spine. He died instantly. The second gunman fired repeatedly at Officer Piagentini, who fell to the sidewalk but, as the gunman cursed him, refused to die. The first gunman then reached down and removed Officer Jones' .38, hefting it in his hand, feeling the weight, as if he were

taking a souvenir, the second gunman wrenched Piagentini's weapon from its holster even as the dying officer flailed at him. Once he had it, he fired every bullet in its chamber into the fallen cop.[279]

Sources regarding the weapons used in the attack have varied. Burrough describes the assailants as armed with pistols. Original press reporting from the *New York Times* said Piagentini and Jones were shot with a .45 caliber submachine gun, similar to the one used a few days earlier to attack Officers Thomas Curry and Nicholas Binetti, who were on guard outside the home of New York District Attorney Frank Hogan, then in the midst of prosecuting the Panther 21 terrorism trial (about which more will be said later).[280] Curry and Binetti were seated in their patrol car outside Hogan's home when a vehicle driving erratically got their attention. Curry and Binetti pursued. When they pulled alongside to direct the driver to pull over, their car was riddled with .45 caliber rounds. Both men were severely injured but survived. The Curry-Binetti attack should also be considered an example of an entrapment style ambush, as reckless driving lured the officers away from their guard position where they could be attacked.

The attacks took place on May 19 and 21, the first date chosen in order to honor the birthday of Malcolm X, as noted in the communique: "[T]he domestic armed forces of racism and oppression will be confronted by the guns of the Black Liberation Army, who will mete out in the tradition of Malcolm and all true revolutionaries real justice. We are revolutionary justice."[281] The message within the package containing the communique delivered to the *Times* noted "the shooting of N.Y.P.D. pigs on Malcolm's birthday."[282] It is worth noting that terrorist attacks and other acts of political violence are frequently conducted on or around dates that are ideologically significant *to the attackers*, not necessarily dates significant to the targets (such as national holidays).

May 19, also the birthday of North Vietnamese Communist leader Ho Chi Minh, also became the name of the BLA's network of allied support (as envisioned by Cleaver), made up of members of the terrorist Weather Underground's New York faction, which called itself the "May 19 Communist Organization" and eventually became the forerunner of the modern anarcho-communist network known as Antifa.²⁸³ The May 19 Communist Organization planted a bomb in the cloakroom of the U.S. Senate in 1983.

The BLA communique claiming responsibility for both attacks included a .45 caliber shell casing from the Curry-Binetti attack. The state of New York eventually prosecuted and successfully convicted BLA leader Dhoruba Moore for the attack, whose fingerprints were found on the communiques. Moore's conviction was overturned in 1990 over allegations of prosecutorial misconduct following revelations of FBI counterintelligence tactics targeting the Black Panthers.

Moore has been both upfront and unapologetic about his role in the BLA. He never repudiated BLA's violence or targeted murder of police officers. He told author Burrough, "The tactical mistake we made was killing the cops in uniform ... when we should've killed the higher-ups. That would've been more effective," a sentiment in keeping with Carlos Marighela's advice.²⁸⁴

Despite Moore's sense of regret for not targeting higher ranking police or their civilian bosses, the entrapment ambush guarantees that the targets will primarily be rank-and-file officers, and it remains a popular attack method today for BIE-motivated perpetrators.

Similar to entrapment ambushes are direct attacks against officers in or near police stations. As with entrapment attacks, assailants are able to lie in wait with confidence that their police targets will be present and distracted on other tasks.

On August 29, 1971, Sergeant John Young was on duty at the Ingleside District Police Station in San Francisco. Most of its officers were out of the area, having responded to a report of a bombing at the Stonestown Mall. Multiple members of the BLA entered the station and opened fire, killing Young and wounding a civilian employee. The attack was reportedly in retaliation for the death of Black Panther field marshal George Jackson, killed during a prison escape attempt. The case went cold but was eventually revived in 1999, taking advantage of new technology in fingerprinting.[285]

Herman Bell and Anthony Bottom, convicted of the Jones and Piagentini murders, pled guilty to Young's murder after more than 40 years. Charges against the remaining defendants were dropped.

BIEs continue to use the threat of explosives serving to lure police into a potential entrapment ambush. In November 2016, four individuals, including one identifying himself as "a member of the Black Panthers," were arrested after planting a bomb on the property of a Trussville, Alabama, elementary school. While the device was made of Play-Doh, wires, and a stopwatch, it did contain gunpowder and so was classified as an explosive. One of the perpetrators, Zachary Edwards, initially told police the intent was to lure police to the elementary school with the bomb threat and then open fire.[286] Police later said the bomb was actually intended to lure police to the elementary school in order to facilitate the armed robbery of a nearby bank, but the robbery was foiled after the would-be robbers spotted a police officer near the bank.[287]

What is considered the most significant attack on a police station during the height of the Black Panthers is not well known. On New Year's Eve, 1972, former navy dental technician Mark Essex waited outside the New Orleans police headquarters for the 11:00 p.m. shift change. He opened fire on the gathered officers and police cadets with a .44 caliber carbine, killing Cadet Alfred Harrell and wounding Lieutenant Horace Perez. Essex then ran through a high crime neighborhood that was notoriously hostile to police and took refuge in a warehouse, where he accidentally triggered a burglar alarm. Two responding K-9 officers, Edwin Hosli Sr. and Harold Blappert, came under fire while exiting their vehicle. Hosli later died of his wounds. Despite a search, Essex escaped. Essex reappeared on January 2, 1973, spotted by a grocer from whom he made a purchase. Police interviewed the grocer, Joseph Perniciaro, about the encounter. Five days later Essex returned and shot Perniciaro for informing on him.

From there, Essex carjacked another individual, traveled to the downtown Howard Johnson hotel that overlooked the New Orleans government building. Upon entering, he shot two hotel patrons and several workers before lighting a fire on the 16th floor and deploying a black liberation flag. While shouting revolutionary and black power slogans, Essex poured gunfire down upon the rapidly establishing police perimeter. Eventually police used a U.S. Marine Corps helicopter to elevate police snipers and enable them to end Essex's standoff. Essex ultimately killed nine people and wounded 12.[288]

Much of the reporting following Essex's mass shooting focused on the killer's experience of racism while serving in San Diego with the U.S. Navy. This is likely in part because Essex's experiences were heavily documented during his court-martial for going AWOL in October 1970. In his propaganda message, signed under the Swahili name Mata (also the Spanish word for "kill") and sent to a New Orleans TV station, Essex also referenced a police shooting of two black students during a protest as the immediate act he was avenging.[289]

Understated in the reporting is that Essex's radicalization coincided with his indoctrination with NOI and Black Power ideology while in San Diego after befriending convicted felon Rodney Frank. Essex was recruited into the Black Panthers in New York City through Black Panther Berenice Jones, who later became Safiyah Bukhari, a member of the BLA and a future leading member of the RNA. Members of the Malcolm X Society established the RNA in Michigan in 1969. Its membership included a number of former RAM leaders. Its objective was to establish the Soviet dream of a separatist black state from Louisiana to South Carolina, and it named Robert F. Williams its first president. In a sense the RNA functioned as the rural component of the FLN-inspired guerilla organization envisioned by Eldridge Cleaver, and there was some cooperation between RNA and BLA cells, especially as police pressure on the BLA mounted.

Essex traveled to New Orleans despite having no history with the city, and he did not affiliate with the local Black Panther chapter.[290] The BLA, however, had a significant base of operations in New Orleans, with a cell conducting bank robberies in the area and a future safe house for BLA fugitive Herman Bell.

The Cleaver branch of the Panthers endorsed Essex's mass shooting. It sent a telegram to Essex's parents reading, "We the Black Panther Party take this opportunity to extend our profound condolences. The loss of your son was a loss to the revolutionary ranks and the black revolutionary struggle as a whole."[291]

All of this raises the question of whether Essex's attack was just one man's response to experienced racism or whether he was recruited, indoctrinated, and instructed to go underground in New Orleans as a member of the BLA.

Comparisons might be drawn between the Essex shooting and Micah Johnson's 2016 Dallas mass shooting in which he murdered five officers. Johnson targeted police at a protest, not at a precinct. But like Essex, Johnson was a former service member with a checkered official record, receiving an honorable discharge only due to an apparent clerical error.[292] Johnson, like Essex, began associating with BIE groups, including the Huey P. Newton Gun Club and the Houston chapter of the New Black Panther Party, although his time affiliating with those groups was relatively short-lived and reportedly stopped before his targeted ambush of police officers.

Johnson fired on police from an elevated position before displacing to a last stand position in which to engage pursuing police.[293] Like Essex, Johnson explicitly said that he wished to shoot whites and specifically targeted white police officers. Johnson also shouted black liberation slogans during the attack, as Essex had done. Hostage negotiator Larry Gordon described Johnson as "very lucid, very sane, and very in control." Upon finding out that Gordon was black, Johnson urged him to turn his weapon on his fellow officers.[294] Ultimately, Johnson wounded 12 and killed five before being killed.[295]

Like Essex, a group with which Johnson had affiliated, the New Black Panther Party, did not claim responsibility but made statements essentially endorsing the attack after the fact.[296]

Following the 2016 Ferguson riots and a number of a high-profile police shootings of black suspects, which the FBI memorandum highlights as beginning the revitalization of BIE activity, a number of armed attacks were conducted on police precincts. Reporting on these attacks has been relatively scarce, and there is minimal public reporting on motivations or affiliations in these attacks.

The Essex attack and the police station assault that killed Officer Young remain outliers. The majority of premediated BLA and Black Panther attacks against police were spontaneous ambushes, usually while an officer was sitting in his patrol car. In a 12-month period between 1972 and 1973, corresponding to the height of the BLA's activities, 56 police officers were ambushed in 33 separate incidents. More than 75 percent of all ambushes took place either while officers were in their cars or in the vicinity of their vehicles.[297]

It is worth noting that while such attacks were "spontaneous," they remained premeditated. The BLA would dispatch its members, typically in small teams of two or three, to find and assassinate police officers. The murder of Atlanta Officer James Greene in November 1971 is a good example of this kind. BLA members Twymon Meyers and Freddie Hilton had just completed a BLA training camp outside of Atlanta and were instructed to find and kill a police officer as a sort of graduation exam. The two gunmen shot Greene at close range with .38 caliber weapons while Greene sat in his patrol car eating a ham biscuit from a nearby late-night eatery.[298] BLA did not claim responsibility for the attack and issued no manifesto or communique.

Following the 2014 Ferguson riots, during the period covered by the FBI's BIE memo, multiple attacks followed a similar pattern to the BLA's spontaneous ambushes.

In October 2014, 32-year-old Zale Thompson wounded two NYPD police officers with a hatchet in a spontaneous ambush before being shot dead. Thompson reportedly attended meetings of the New Black Panther Party. A leader of the group hailed Thompson as a "crusader" but denied he had ever been a member.[299] Thompson was also known to have converted to Islam and reportedly spent time studying jihadist websites. Thompson had a large playlist of speeches featuring former Black Panther and SNCC leader H. Rap Brown, now known as Jamil

Abdullah Amin, the leader of a black Islamist sect known as al-Ummah.[300]

The DOJ identified al-Ummah as "a group that is alleged to have engaged in violent activity over a period of many years and known to be armed" and consists of "a group of mostly African-American converts to Islam, which seeks to establish a separate Sharia-law governed state within the United States." Amin is currently serving time in a Colorado supermax prison for the murder of a law enforcement officer.[301]

In December 2014, Ismaaiyl Brinsley, an Atlanta resident, travelled to Baltimore, Maryland, where he shot and wounded an ex-girlfriend.[302] He then travelled to New York City, where he ambushed and killed two NYPD officers, Wenjian Liu and Rafael Ramos, while they sat in their patrol car. Shortly before the attack Brinsley posted on social media that he was "putting wings on pigs today" in language reminiscent of '70s-era Black Panther propaganda. Brinsley also referenced the deaths of Eric Garner and Michael Brown, two black men killed in confrontations with police.[303] Following the attack Brinsley fled to a subway station and, after being engaged by police, killed himself.[304]

NYPD investigators pursued leads that Brinsley's attack may have been connected to threats made by the BGF based in part on Brinsley's time in Baltimore, a well-known hub of BGF activity. Reports of potential attacks against police originating from Baltimore had appeared on law enforcement's radar on November 25 and again on December 5 prior to the attack.[305] A federal law enforcement source later denied a BGF connection.[306] There were also indicators that Brinsley held Islamic religious views and may have attended a mosque historically linked to Al Qaeda finance.[307]

Bombings and Hijackings

Targeted assassination of police officers was the primary form of terrorism adopted by Black Panther/BLA perpetrators but were not the only terrorism crimes committed. Other examples of criminal acts associated with terrorism, including bombings and hijackings, were also carried out during this period.

One of the earliest such incidents was the 1965 attempted bombing of the Statute of Liberty by members of the Black Liberation Front, a group led by then 28-year-old library clerk named Robert Steele Collier, nicknamed "Fidelismo." Collier had recently traveled to Cuba and was known by the FBI to be associated with RAM and to have attended meetings of the OAAU, the organization formed by Malcolm X after his split from the NOI.[308] Like New Orleans Black Panther mass shooter Mark Essex, Collier had a brief and unimpressive military background, receiving a less than honorable discharge from the U.S. Navy following a number of events, including nearly provoking an international incident in France and stabbing a woman while stationed in England.[309]

The conspiracy sought to decapitate the Statute of Liberty and destroy other American monuments including the Liberty Bell using dynamite procured from members of the FLQ, a Cuban-backed Quebec separatist group. One of the members of the Black Liberation Front group was an undercover New York Police officer, however, and shortly after the Canadian smuggler delivered the dynamite, the whole group was arrested.[310]

While nothing is explicitly stated in the FBI records, it seems reasonable that Cuban intelligence may have played a role in connecting Collier with the Canadians who supplied the explosives. Michelle Duclos, who smuggled the explosives, was introduced to Collier through another Quebec separatist he met during his trip to Cuba. Duclos was a regular to the United Nations scene in New York, which was the center of Cuban operations in North America given that Cuba had no embassy or consulates in the United States and the New York mission to the U.N. provided diplomatic immunity for Cuban intelligence officers. Collier traveled in similar U.N circles, meeting Ernesto "Che" Guevara during the Cuban revolutionary's trip to the United Nations.[311] David Mitchell in the *Journal of Counterterrorism and Homeland Security* calls accusations that the Cubans may have had a hand in the plot "highly speculative" but "not entirely without merit."[312]

Collier and his compatriots received relatively short sentences, which would be further reduced. Mitchell records:

> Collier, Bowe, and Sayyed had all been found guilty on both counts of plotting to destroy government property and the smuggling of explosives. Collier's sentence was reduced in November 1965 to 5 years in prison followed by 5 years probation. He served only 2 years before being paroled on 22 March 1967. Bowe's sentence was reduced to 3 years in prison followed by 3 years probation, and Sayyed's was reduced to 18 months in prison followed by 2 years probation.[313]

After his release, Collier curiously enough played a role as a defendant in yet another bombing conspiracy case in April 1969. This became known as the Panther 21 trial, one of the most contentious trials of the decade. According to early reports, 21 members of the New York chapter of the Black Panther Party—including Collier, who was identified as a Black Panther minister of education—had hoped to orchestrate a bombing campaign targeting police stations, railways, and department stores.

Among those indicted were future BLA leaders Sekou Odinga, Dhorba Moore, Lumumba Shakur, and Donald Weems (aka Kuwasi Balagoon).[314] The Black Panthers' second-in-command, Bobby Seale, was also charged in the plot.[315] In addition to the prospective department store bombings, the conspirators were charged with a planned bombing/sniper attack against a Bronx police station and the failed bombing of a Queens school district office building.[316] The lengthy two-year trial was subsumed in a media circus, and the defendants were supported by a who's who of New York society, as memorialized in Tom Wolfe's essay where he coined the phrase *Radical Chic*.[317]

Defense attorneys argued entrapment, claiming that NYPD informants and undercover police officers played an outside role in the conspiracy, and the jury returned a quick verdict of not guilty—even for those Panthers who had jumped bail and fled to Algeria to join Eldridge Cleaver in avoiding arrest.[318]

Given that the New York Panthers were soon to become the BLA and unleash a tide of murder against police for the next several years, it is easy to find New York prosecutors' claims to be credible that the Panthers intended to launch wave of violence against police. This is particularly true when one considers that the same bombing and police station assault technique alleged in the Panther 21 case was subsequently used in the attack that led to the death of Sergeant Young. Still, it remains an article of faith among many police critics that the Panther 21 case represented a textbook example of entrapment.

Such arguments do not always win the day, however. In 2015, Olajuwon Ali Davis, 23, and Brandon Orlando Baldwin, 24, were convicted on weapons charges for seeking to acquire weapons and explosives to carry out a bombing of the St. Louis Gateway Arch and a police station. These bombings were reportedly to serve as a distraction to facilitate the assassination of then-St. Louis County Prosecuting Attorney Robert P. McCulloch and then-Ferguson Police Chief Thomas Jackson.

According to *St. Louis Today*, both men were affiliated with the St. Louis chapter of the New Black Panther Party:

> Investigators previously identified both defendants as members of the St. Louis Chapter of the New Black Panther Party. Baldwin also is known as Brandon Muhammad, according to court documents, and Davis also uses the last name Ali and goes by Brother Ali. Baldwin described himself as a field marshal for the party, his plea says. Davis said that he once carried a gun as part of a security detail for the party. Davis spoke in October at a New Black Panther rally at the

Greater St. Mark Family Church about the killing of Brown. Davis was identified that day as the Missouri chapter's "minister of law."[319]

Reports also note that Davis identified himself as a "Moorish-American" and posted videos describing how Moors could avoid paying taxes.[320] Both Davis and Baldwin pled guilty.[321]

As in the Panther 21 case, media representatives hurried to shape the narrative landscape, with one outlet describing the conspiracy as "The Black Panther Bomb Plot in St. Louis That Wasn't."[322] Even after Davis was released from prison, media coverage of the would-be bomber remains glowing, treating the two convicted Black Panthers as victims of a government conspiracy and detailing the highlights of Davis's new career as stage actor.[323] Curiously, this post-prison reputation rehabilitation is another common part of Panther history. After Robert Steele Collier was released from prison for the 1965 Statue of Liberty plot, his first job was also for a theatrical company. An anonymous donor eventually paid his salary to direct a community center in Manhattan, where he was tasked with recruiting over 700 area "youths" for various community projects. Eventually he was made the director of a New York City government recreation center, even as the FBI kept Collier on a list of "potential bombing suspects."[324]

Is the FBI concerned with the possibility of recidivism among modern Panther perpetrators? According to one post-prison feature article, the FBI's post-prison interview with Davis focused on "What could we [the FBI] have done to prevent you from going down this path of violence?"[325]

Bombings remain a potential method with a long historical track record among Black Panther inspired BIEs. Airplane hijackings, which came into vogue in the late 1960s and early 1970s as the premier terrorism method, are probably not likely to see a resurgence given modern advancements in security.

Inspired by high-profile skyjackings conducted by Marxist terrorists such the PFLP, a number of Black Panthers and related black liberation adherents attempted to hijack jetliners to facilitate escapes, raise funds for the movement, or demand the release of arrested comrades. Many of the crimes were premised on the notion that Cuba or Algeria would welcome Black Panther hijackers, a belief that had mixed results in practice.

In 1965, former SNCC member and Black Panther Lorenzo Edward "Kom'boa" Ervin Jr. seized an Eastern Airlines flight from Atlanta to San Juan. Armed with a .38 caliber pistol, he redirected the flight to Cuba. Cuban authorities, however, did not allow Ervin to remain, and he was forced to continue on to Czechoslovakia. Eventually sold out by the Cubans, Ervin was returned to the United States to face a life sentence for hijacking and kidnapping. While in prison, Ervin became an exponent of anarchism and a foremost thinker in black liberation from an anarchist perspective (about which more will be said later). He was released in 1984.[326]

On June 3, 1972, Vietnam veteran and Black Panther Roger Holder and his girlfriend Cathy Kerkow hijacked Western Airlines Flight 701, using a briefcase with protruding wires. They demanded and received $500,000 and the release of Black Panther Angela Davis from prison. Davis, implicated in buying the murder weapon used to kill a California judge but acquitted of criminal responsibility, was being held on charges related to an attempted jail break of Black Panther field marshal George Jackson before flying to Algeria. They received the money, but Davis would not join them (she was found not guilty and released shortly afterward). The two hijackers smoked marijuana and had sex during the flight. Upon arrival in Algiers, the Algerian government seized the money. Holder eventually fled to Paris before finally turning himself in to police and returning to the United States for trial. Kerkow remains on the FBI's most wanted list of domestic terrorists.[327]

The July 1972 BLA hijacking of Delta Flight 841 had similar mixed results. Led by George Wright, a convicted armed robber who had recently escaped from minimum security prison, the group of five self-described BLA members seized control of the plane with a pistol concealed inside a hollowed-out Bible with Wright dressed as a priest. The hijackers demanded the FBI pay them $1 million when the plane touched down in Miami, which the Bureau did. They then traveled to Boston, took on an international navigator, and flew to Algiers. Upon arrival, Algerian authorities seized the money, which they returned to the FBI, but allowed the hijackers to remain in Algeria.[328] As relations between Algeria and the United States eventually thawed, several of the hijackers fled to France, where they lived until captured by French police. France refused to extradite the subjects to the United States but held them in a French prison.[329] Wright was identified living in Portugal, but the Portuguese government refused extradition. Wright, like Kerkow, remains on the list of the FBI's most wanted domestic terrorists.[330]

Most of the Black Panther and BLA forays into hijacking lacked both the professionalism and the bloodthirstiness of those conducted by Soviet-backed Marxist groups such as the PFLP and Germany's Red Army Faction. Even so, it shows how Black Panther/BLA members were influenced by trends in terrorism operations and were willing and able to adapt to new methods.

Chapter Six:
Black Lives Matter and Other Modern Marxist BIE Incarnations

Formation and Ideology
Dragon or Hydra?

The dichotomy between the theatrical, provocative, and centrally organized Black Panther Party and the autonomous, secretive, and bloody-minded BLA is a useful taxonomy for understanding many modern Marxist BIE organizations.

Most groups, even those not explicitly founded as successors to these groups, tend to display traits comparable to one or the other even while displaying ideological or organizational elements of both. For example, the New Black Panther Party, the Huey P. Newton Gun Club, and the NFAC can all be seen through the Newton-led Black Panther Party paradigm. In public, they primarily operate within the law, emphasizing public demonstrations, often while heavily armed, with matching militant uniforms and paramilitary-style hierarchical organization. They are typically led by a single charismatic and stylistically ostentatious individual who is readily available for media interviews. While individuals associated with these groups have engaged in acts of premeditated violence, the groups themselves do not claim responsibility for these attacks and usually deny any relation to the perpetrators.

In contrast, the Revolutionary Abolitionist Movement (not to be confused with the 1960s Revolutionary Action Movement, although the similarity is probably not a coincidence) is a deliberately autonomous, independently organized group consisting of local and regional clandestine cells. This group calls the BLA "the most successful guerrilla movement in the US in the 20th Century" after which it has clearly modeled itself.[331] The Revolutionary Abolitionist Movement embraces the autonomous and cellular structure of the BLA that Cleaver insisted upon while believing that this time it will overcome the challenges of previous underground groups whose lack of above-ground support elements resulted in significant, if politically ineffectual, violence.

RAM has no publicly identifiable membership. Anonymous masked members do occasionally pose with firearms or provide interviews to radical media outlets. Their indoctrination and training program, the Kuwasi Balagoon Liberation School, is named after former BLA terrorist Donald Weems, who was convicted and sentenced to prison for his role in the 1981 Brinks armored car robbery.[332]

Weems became one of a cohort of very influential black anarchists while in prison. Other former BLA or BPPSD members-turned-anarchists include Lorenzo Kom'boa, who authored the seminal work *Anarchism and the Black Revolution*, and Russell "Maroon" Shoatz, a BLA member convicted of murdering Philadelphia Police Sergeant Frank Von Colln.

Shoatz is the author of *The Dragon and the Hydra*, in which he examines the difficulty of leadership in the black liberation struggle. Shoatz appropriated the terms *dragon* and *hydra* to refer to the different orientation of black liberation organizations along the lines we described, contrasting dispersed leaderless rebellions as "hydras" with strict hierarchical groups organized around charismatic leaders he referred to as "dragons." He warned that "dragons" are particularly susceptible to being coopted by their imperialist opponents and often exhibit dictatorial tendencies that eventually end up destroying a revolutionary group, while he lauded the success of leaderless "hydras." Shoatz wrote:

> Therefore, the global hardships brought about by today's imperialists and their voracious accumulation of wealth, and their destruction of the environment and

cultures will propel the multitudes to use any and all means to bring about the needed changes—or perish. And modern means of communications will provide them with the means to both update and imitate the earlier hydra's strengths, avoid its weaknesses—while guarding against the tendency of the dragons to concentrate oppressive power in its hands.

Thus, since both the shared needs and necessity for change is already present, along with the tools to communicate, then our final consideration is whether or not these masses must centralize their organizing (not to be confused with the obvious need to coordinate their efforts!). To that I answer with an emphatic, 'no!' and further, I contend that such centralization will only make it easier for our oppressors to identify and level repression upon us—prolonging the crisis our generation must deal with.[333]

Curiously, while Shoatz never mentioned the name in the piece, the critique of charismatic revolutionary figureheads brings to mind Black Panther field marshal George Jackson, whose famous last words during his failed prison escape were "Gentlemen, the Dragon has come."[334] One cannot help but wonder if this association was not intentional on Shoatz's part. Through Shoatz, one can see that the fundamental conflict between proponents of above- and underground activities, as well as centralized versus decentralized organization, remains as deeply engrained as in the days of Newton and Cleaver.

Shoatz himself received compassionate release from prison just prior to passing away in December 2021, which may have played a role in his becoming an increasingly cited figure.

But Shoatz's critique also surely resonates in the wake of the 2020 George Floyd uprising, as many black radical activists criticized the role played by official Black Lives Matter organizations, such as the

Black Lives Matter Global Network Foundation (BLMGNF) during the events of that summer, accusing the group of abandoning revolutionary action in favor of self-aggrandizement.[335]

Trained Marxists

One of the challenges in discussing the nature and scope of Black Lives Matter has been the inherent nebulousness of the slogan. Is BLM a movement, a network, or an organization? When specific individuals or organizations associated with BLM face criticism, supporters commonly fall back upon the generally unobjectionable statement inherent in the name rather than address specific allegations. As Robert Stilson of the Capital Research Center notes:

> The upshot of this is that the structure of Black Lives Matter means something different depending on what part of the movement is being referenced. To the person using it on social media or the protestor writing it on a sign, it might simply reflect that individual's anger at events such as George Floyd's killing or serve as a way of expressing support for policy changes. But this ambiguity can cause confusion among observers and commentators when decentralized movements are conflated with actual existing legal entities that accept tax-deductible donations.[336]

When discussing the nuts and bolts of BLM, however, most are referring specifically to two interlocking organizations, BLMGNF and the Movement for Black Lives (M4BL).[337]

What is generally agreed upon is that the original name, and the group that eventually became BLMGNF, was created by three black women—Alicia Garza, Opal Tometi, and Patrisse Cullors—in the summer of 2013 following the acquittal of George Zimmerman in the self-defense shooting death of Trayvon Martin. The group was then supercharged by its participation in the Ferguson protest/riots the subsequent year. M4BL was also founded out of Ferguson as a sort of umbrella organization that covered multiple participants in the protests and came to be called the "heart of the uprising."[338]

The statement by BLM founder Cullors that she and her colleagues were "trained Marxists" would be breathlessly reported by conservative media outlets all throughout 2020. But as Heritage Foundation senior fellow Mike Gonzalez demonstrates in his book *BLM: The Making of a New Marxist Revolution*, this admission was, if anything, a major understatement:

> Even before [BLM founders Garza, Cullors, and Tometi] created the hashtag expression #BlackLivesMatter in 2013, that later became an empire of revolutionary organizations around the world, they belonged or associated with an interlacing web of socialist groups that have been trying to overthrow the American system for decades.[339]

In addition to having a devotion to BLA fugitive cop-killer Assata Shakur, BLA leaders drew on perennial CPUSA presidential candidate and former Black Panther Angela Davis for inspiration, as well as anarcho-feminist icon bell hooks (who does not capitalize her name in keeping with an anarchist practice).[340] More concretely, both Cullors and Garza were raised in elite high schools with Marxist curricula designed to indoctrinate revolutionaries, where they were identified by teachers and admitted into activist training camps.[341] This familiar pattern of recruitment mirrors that of SNCC chairman and Black Panther Stokely Carmichael and his own time at the Bronx School of Science with the scion of Communist Party leadership. From here both women joined radical organizing groups. For Cullors, that place was the Labor/Community Strategy Center, a training center founded by former Weather Underground member Eric Mann, which she would come to call "home" and where she would remain for at least a decade.[342]

Mann's revolutionary C.V. is top-notch. Recruited by SNCC members straight out of college, Mann served as an organizer for the Congress on Racial Equality, eventually joined the Weather Underground faction that seized control of the Students for a Democracy Society and participated in the Weather Underground's efforts at violent revolution. Mann served 18 months in prison for his part in a shooting attack on a Cambridge, Massachusetts, police station in 1969.[343] After prison, Mann continued his professional organizing career, including working at as a union organizer for the Maoist League of Revolutionary Struggle (LRS) from 1975 to 1985, a conglomeration of a various ethnic Communist groups that eventually dissolved in 1990 during the Soviet collapse,[344] with elements of the LRS later joining the Freedom Road Socialist Organization (FRSO).[345] As Mann explains, LRS continued to maintain the old Soviet obsession with establishing a Black homeland in the deep South:

> The LRS envisioned a socialist revolution in the United States as part of a world revolution in which a black nation in the American South and a Chicano nation in the Southwest would ally with the multinational working class—including white workers—and the peoples and nations of the Third World.[346]

LRS's deep connection to this traditional Marxist project is perhaps unsurprising, as one of its leaders included well-known Marxist playwright Amira Baraka, who served on the LRS's Central Committee and as editor of its newspaper *Black Nation*.[347] Baraka was a contemporary and associate of Robert F. Williams and traveled with Williams to Cuba as a member of the Fair Play for Cuba Committee in 1960.[348]

Alicia Garza was also recruited into FRSO through its front, the School for Unity and Liberation. From there Garza pinballed among other FRSO fronts, including People United for a Better Life in Oakland and Leftroots.³⁴⁹ She also worked closely with the Chinese Progressive Association (CPA), a front for I Wor Kuen, a Maoist organization and one of the founding organizations of LRS.³⁵⁰ The CPA later also served as the fiscal sponsor for Garza's Black Futures Lab organizing project.³⁵¹ Heritage's Gonzalez told the *Washington Times* that the "CPA works with China's communist government, pushes its agenda here in the United States and is regularly praised by China's state-owned mouthpieces."³⁵²

Another significant LRS/FRSO tie to the Black Lives Matter network is the Organization for Black Struggle, the St. Louis–based organization that played a key role in organizing the first BLM protests in Ferguson in 2014 and derives its agenda from the FRSO-instituted Black Radical Congress Freedom Agenda.³⁵³

M4BL is an umbrella organization of between 50 and 150 member groups, according to the coalition website. These organizations include BLMGNF as well as the Organization for Black Struggle.³⁵⁴ M4BL also has very interesting ties to historical Communist organizations, particularly internationally.

From its founding until 2021, M4BL's fiscal sponsor (the tax-deductible nonprofit through which the M4BL receives donations) was the Alliance for Global Justice (AfGJ). As this author testified before the U.S. Senate Judiciary Committee Subcommittee on the Constitution:

> Alliance for Global Justice describes itself as founded by the 'Nicaragua Network,' an organization devoted to supporting 'an armed revolution.' The Nicaragua Network was founded as a U.S.-based 'solidarity committee' under the direction of the Soviet-backed, Marxist-Leninist Sandinista National Liberation Front (FSLN) which took power in 1979. A parallel solidarity committee for the communist Farabundo Marti National Liberation Front (FMLN) guerrillas of El Salvador, known as CISPES, is known to have been

under Cuban intelligence direction and part of an array of international front organizations vertically integrated into Soviet active measures campaigns against the United States in the 1980s. The Nicaragua Network faced accusations of failing to register as a foreign agent but was never convicted. Some of its American operatives were later found to have been connected with the FARC narcoguerrillas of Colombia.[355]

Further connecting AfGJ to Cuba and Latin American Communism is its fiscal sponsorship of the Venceremos Brigade,[356] an operation formed in 1969 to recruit American students for Cuban intelligence, according to Cuban defector Gerardo Peraza.[357] Members of BLM traveled to Cuba with the 46th Venceremos Brigade,[358] whose slogan "From Harlem to Havana" further emphasized a connection.[359] Following a 2021 outbreak of protests against the Communist government, both M4BL and BLMGNF issued statements in support of the Cuban government.[360]

In January 2021, M4BL dropped AfGJ as a fiscal sponsor and replaced it with the Common Counsel Foundation.[361] Perhaps not coincidentally, the foundation's executive director, Peggy Saika, is close to the CPA, serving on the host committee of the group's 40th anniversary event, which also received donations from FRSO and Eric Mann's Labor/Community Strategy Center.[362]

BLM has also maintained close ties to the regime of Venezuelan President Nicholas Maduro, who has clung to power in large part due to Cuba's capable security and intelligence services.[363] During the 2020 George Floyd uprising, federal officials alleged that the Maduro regime was playing a role in instigating violence during BLM protests, as the *Miami Herald* reported:

> We are aware of efforts by individuals linked to America's adversaries, including the illegitimate

regime of Venezuela's Nicolas Maduro, to instigate conflict, help incite violence, and divide Americans by exploiting peaceful protests.[364]

According to former CIA officer Gary Bernsten, a Venezuelan intelligence defector alleged that the Venezuelan regime funded up to $10 million of BLM's startup costs, a covert operation that followed BLM's Opal Tometi's visit the South American state in 2013, using proceeds from narcotrafficking.[365]

In March 2020, DOJ indicted Maduro and 14 other Venezuelan officials for their role in FARC narcotrafficking, noting, "As alleged, Maduro and the other defendants expressly intended to flood the United States with cocaine in order to undermine the health and wellbeing of our nation. Maduro very deliberately deployed cocaine as a weapon."[366]

For her part, Tometi maintained close ties with the Venezuelan regime, returning in 2015 to serve as an election monitor.[367] She also joined Maduro on a panel in Harlem during an event to fete the Venezuelan dictator.[368] In December 2015, Tometi penned a letter opposing U.S. efforts at "counterrevolution" in Venezuela and offered "unwavering solidarity with the progressive and revolutionary Venezuelan people."[369]

Revolutionary Grift?

As significant as the alleged $10 million from Venezuelan sources may have been to BLM's start, that amount was rapidly dwarfed by the tremendous amounts of money that flowed into the organization during the 2020 violent uprising across the United States. The Claremont Institute's Center for the American Way produced a comprehensive database cataloguing corporate pledges to the BLM movement and related causes. It found that the BLM organization took in $123 million from 2020 to 2023.[370] Of that $123 million, at least $90 million was raised in 2020 alone, according to a BLM annual report from that year.[371] The organization reportedly distributed $21.7 million to its various chapters and allied groups, while its own operating costs were $8.4 million the same year, with the remaining $60 million or so unaccounted for.

By 2022, the BLM network was reportedly "in the red," with a deficit of $9 million,[372] despite having given out only a third of the funds it had previously accumulated.[373] Some of those funds were reportedly diverted for corrupt or unethical purposes, with Cullors going on a $3.2 million real estate purchasing spree of four homes since 2016.[374] Millions of dollars were reportedly also redirected to family members and associates of Cullors who served as vendors for services ranging from "consulting" to "security."[375]

While much of the criticism of BLMGNF and Cullors personally has focused on the allegedly corrupt financial aspect, much of the opposition internally had more to do with political power structures.

Initially, BLM emphasized its decentralized nature, and, particularly during the 2020 uprising, BLM was largely represented by its dozens of local and largely autonomous chapters. But as the fires in the streets cooled and as money flowed in, power became centralized. Beginning in November 2020, a group of 10 BLM chapters expressed concerns about this centralization, saying that local BLM affiliates were being passed over for the distribution of funds and not consulted on issues of policy. BLMGNF launched a political action committee and began focusing on national political concerns—including election get-out-the-vote efforts and passing legislation—rather than engaging in radical political organizing in black communities. A statement by the so-called #BLM10 expressed their concerns, saying:

> Chapters are autonomous and have their own infrastructure, governance, and are organized based on the uniqueness of their local contexts. Our

Chapters each base our work on changing the material conditions of Black people where we are. Member chapters have been fully entrenched in their own local struggles, confronting municipal power brokers and doing the dangerous work of facing off against the police.

Because BLMGN was not engaged in direct organizing, it had resources available to do other things, such as engage with media, foundations and power brokers of the systems we are fighting against to present our local work as their own.

With their time and resources, our local campaigns were co-opted under the BLMGN banner, which assumed credit for our work, and consolidated credibility, power, and resources into an opaque institution. As a result of our statement last year BLMGN released an Impact Statement for the first time in its existence. The Impact Statement exposed what we have long argued: the primary "liberation" operations of BLMGN are currently social media campaigns and corporate partnerships, not on the ground organizing, campaigns or protests.[376]

One cannot help but note the local chapters referring to their work of "facing off against the police."

The background of BLM's founders, and their public statements about Assata Shakur, might have suggested an organizing approach closer to the BLA than the BPPSD. But after 2020, the historical tension between "dragons" and "hydras" once again reasserted itself.

Cullors was eventually forced out of her position as chief executive of BLMGNF although the organization's website still honors her as a founder. Twenty-five BLM chapters sued BLMGNF, seeking access to funds allegedly denied them.[377] The organization also faced official action as multiple state governments announced that the nonprofit was out of compliance with regulations and would not be permitted to conduct further fundraising within their jurisdictions.[378]

BLM's internal strife amid allegations of corruption and self-dealing bears a striking resemblance to the BPPSD following Huey P. Newton's successful 1971 release from prison, with an emphasis less on ideological purity and more on a variety of "programs" from which funds were extracted from BPPSD supporters for Newton's personal empire.

BLM and Law Enforcement

For BLM's interactions with law enforcement, including its role in the 2020 George Floyd uprising, rather than either Newton's BPPSD or Cleaver's BLA, perhaps the more accurate comparison might be the Stokely Carmichael–led SNCC. As with the SNCC, BLM's position as a high-status position as a civil rights organization helped the media ignore the role the organization played in inciting deadly violence.

"Defund the Police" versus Abolition

To say that the BLM relationship with law enforcement is acrimonious would be an understatement.

BLM appears to have initiated calls to "defund the police" as a means of reducing police budgets across the country through political pressure. Indeed, following violent riots during the George Floyd uprising, several major cities responded to that call. They reduced police budgets[379] with disastrous effects on crime rates, which correspondingly surged.[380]

What is not widely understood is that even this "defund" position itself represented a media-friendly moderation of BLM's actual position, which is for the complete abolition of all police and all prisons. The BLMGNF continues to host on its website a multi-part video series featuring BLM founder Patrisse Cullors entitled "Imagining Abolition."[381] In response to calls for "defunding" police, one organizer wrote a *New York Times* op-ed rejecting police "reform" and insisting, "Yes, We Mean Literally Abolish the Police."[382]

Self-described abolitionists define their target as "the carceral state" or the "prison industrial complex," a term coined by former Black Panther and Communist Party leader Angela Davis. Professor Ruby Tapia defines the "carceral state" as including

> the formal institutions and operations and economies of the criminal justice system proper, but it also encompasses logics, ideologies, practices, and structures, that invest in tangible and sometimes intangible ways in punitive orientations to difference, to poverty, to struggles to social justice and to the crossers of constructed borders of all kinds.[383]

Carceral, referring to incarceration, is not an English word. It is borrowed from French socialist philosopher Michel Foucault's observation that "everything is carceral."[384] While often cloaked in language reminiscent of the fight for the abolition of slavery more than 200 years earlier, such as alleging that professionalized policing began with "slave patrols," in reality the concept of abolitionism put forward by BLM has more in common with the anarchist and Marxist language of "abolition of the state." As Wayne Price writes in *The Abolition of the State: Anarchist and Marxist Perspectives*, policing and incarceration are seen as the central element without which the state cannot exist:

> The dominant power of a territory, the state is a bureaucratic-military machine standing above, and alienated from, the rest of class-divided society, serving

the interests of the upper class. In *The Origins of the Family, Private Property, and the State*, Engels describes it as a "public force" which "consists not merely of armed men but also of material appendages, prisons, and coercive institutions of all kinds...." (1972; p. 230). Its officials are "organs of society standing above society ... representatives of a power which estranges them from society.... The state is an organization for the protection of the possessing class against the non-possessing class" (p. 231).

In the anarchist classic, *The State, Its Historic Role,* Peter Kropotkin writes, similarly, "The State ... includes the existence of a power situated above society ... the concentration in the hands of a few of many functions in the life of societies.... A whole mechanism of legislation and of policing has to be developed in order to subject some classes to the domination of others" (1987; p. 10).

Thus, the Anarchist/Marxist definition of *the state* and the modern concept of the "carceral state" can been seen as essentially the same. This is why BLMGNF claimed on its website that one of its goals was to "disrupt the Western-prescribed nuclear family structure requirement,"[385] which from a Marxist perspective can be understood as one of Engels's "coercive institutions."

Many wonder why working to overthrow the Constitution, though a crime, is often permitted in the United States. Under Title 18, Section 2385, of the *U.S. Code*, and under the codes of many states, it is unlawful to advocate (which by definition requires more than mere speech but a bevy of significant organizing activities) for the overthrow of the U.S. federal government or the various state governments.[386] However, due to established legal precedents, including *Pennsylvania v. Nelson* and *Yates v. United States*, these codes are largely considered unenforceable today.[387]

There is a somewhat related statute in Section 2384, called "seditious conspiracy," that is enforceable, however. Seditious conspiracy is a conspiracy by two or more persons to use force to overthrow the U.S. government or a state government, or an attempt to seize a government building (federal, state, or local) by force of arms for similar purpose. Former federal prosecutor Andrew McCarthy explains that such a charge has nothing to do with First Amendment rights:

> Similarly, if there is evidence that people are using force or plotting violent attacks against U.S. government installations, there is no viable objection to the introduction of evidence that they hated the United States and called for attacks against the government. The statements are not the crime; they are evidence of the crime, and the First Amendment does not prohibit their use as such. Judges, moreover, carefully instruct juries that people may not be convicted for holding unpopular beliefs; there must be proof beyond a reasonable doubt, in a seditious-conspiracy case, that they conspired to use force against the nation and its government. That's the crime.[388]

Primary targets for the George Floyd uprising included police precincts such as the one in Minneapolis that was seized and burned and one in Seattle that police were forced to abandon in the city's so-called Capitol Hill Autonomous Zone. Other government installations that came under sustained attack include the Mark O. Hatfield Federal Courthouse in Portland, Oregon, which was besieged nightly for nearly two months,[389] and the White House, where massive unlawful protests and attempts to force entry into the presidential compound forced President Trump into a secure underground bunker.[390]

In 2020, Attorney General William Barr argued for U.S. district attorneys using the seditious conspiracy statute in response to the

2020 uprising, a position for which he received substantial media criticism. No such charges were ever filed.[391]

To what extent were BLM's abolitionist policies the motive for violence in 2020?

BLM and Rioting

If one accepts that the BLM movement's ultimate goal is the abolition of the state (by initial means of the abolition of police to enforce the laws), then the question of whether BLM bears responsibility for the violence emanating out of the protests held in its name becomes significant. Much critical ink has been spilt over the question of whether those events were "mostly peaceful."[392]

Mike Gonzalez argues that BLM played an outsized role in the events of 2020:

> That BLM was deeply involved in driving people to protests and riots after Floyd's death can be seen in BLM's own 2020 impact report released March 2021. "The average open rate for nonprofit emails is about 25%. In early June, our email providing event and safety resources to people wanting to mobilize saw a 63% open rate," it boasted, using "event and safety" clearly as a euphemism for mobilizing protestors.[393]

It has been argued that, given the large number of total protests conducted in 2020, most were non-violent. As a statistical matter that may be true, but it is highly misleading. The Major Cities Chiefs Association documented over 8,700 protest events in the 68 major cities that responded to its survey, with the total number of protests significantly higher. While the majority of those protests did not include acts of violence, only 51 percent of protests were both peaceful and lawful. Of the responding agencies, 94 percent reported dealing with non-violent but illegal protests (such as blockading roadways), and 79 percent of agencies experienced at least one protest featuring acts of violence.[394] Most violence consisted of attacks on police officers, along with looting and arson:

> Approximately, 72% of major city law enforcement agencies had officers harmed during the protests. This included nearly every agency that experienced at least one violent protest. In total, over the course of the civil unrest from May to July, more than 2,000 officers sustained injuries in the line of duty. One agency reported 50 officers being injured in a single week of protests. Another agency reported that 462 of their officers were injured during the protests in their jurisdiction.[395]

Property Claims Services, which tracks insurance claims, reported that the 2020 riots cost insurance companies between $1 billion and $2 billion worth of damage.[396] That figure likely does not include additional costs from businesses or individuals who were uninsured or underinsured or who had other reasons for not reporting the damage. At least 25 people were killed in the political unrest, including protestors and bystanders.[397]

To what extent was BLM responsible for that damage? Gonzalez cites *The Federalist*'s Joy Pullman, who, in examining data from the Armed Conflict Location and Event Data Project, noted, "BLM activists were involved in 95 percent of the riots for which there is information about the perpetrators' affiliation."[398]

Following the race riots between 1965 and 1968 (of which the SNCC played an inciting part in several), the U.S. Senate conducted a series of extensive hearings regarding the violence, which were ultimately published in a 23-volume series of reports:

> Senate investigators commissioned a survey of more

than 137 affected cities to calculate incidents of arson, looting, sniper fire, and police and civilian deaths and injuries. They interviewed police, intelligence personnel, professional researchers, and non-profit leaders, about the nature of militant groups. They spoke on a bipartisan basis to mayors and local government leaders about their experiences and local and state efforts to improve urban living conditions, lessen racial tensions, and mitigate agitation from militants.[399]

Will there ever be such an extensive investigation into the 2020 riots? Despite calls by the National Police Association for just such an inquiry, and surveys showing that 66 percent of Americans favor an investigation into the riots, such a detailed examination of that violent summer must be regarded as ultimately unlikely.[400] But absent such an investigation, the full extent of BLM's responsibility will remain elusive.

Conclusion

On April 12, 2021, 63-year-old Frank James boarded a New York City subway train while wearing a vest and hard hat associated with New York transit employees. Once aboard he donned a gas mask, deployed a smoke grenade, and began opening fire on passengers with a handgun. James discharged 33 rounds, ultimately wounding 10 people.

James was caught 30 hours later and charged with terrorism against a mass transit system[401] and eventually pled guilty. None of the DOJ press releases involving James's indictment or conviction mentioned his motive in the attack—despite the fact that motive is a necessary legal component of proving terrorism offenses.

But material posted to James's social media pages included images and text linked to black identity extremist ideologies, including the Nation of Islam, Moorish Science, Black Panthers, Black Liberation Army, and Black Lives Matter. He notably posted a picture of Micah Johnson, the BLM supporter who killed 5 Dallas police officers in 2016. In online videos James can be seen urging racial separatism between whites and blacks.[402]

Furthermore, *Newsweek*'s Tom O'Connor reported that James had actually come to the attention of the FBI in 2019 but had been "cleared."[403] Here, in the social media of a single attacker, were links and threads from all of the significant BIE groups documented in this work. Yet the FBI, which coined the very term *Black Identity Extremism* only to abandon it under political pressure, was unable to recognize the nature of that extremism for what it was when it examined James's social media two years prior to his terrorist attack. James was thus another "known wolf" mass shooter.[404]

Because of the nature of today's digital world, which provides individuals with a far greater access to various ideas, it is increasingly likely that police will find offenders who have associated, or dabbled in the beliefs of, multiple BIE groups, as James apparently did. If perpetrators are deriving meaning from the symbols and documents of a wider variety of groups, it will be increasingly relevant for investigators to recognize and coherently describe the nature and motivations of those groups, both historical and modern, to have the knowledge and expertise necessary to interpret what they are seeing, and to determine the implications of those beliefs in a perpetrator's behavior.

As we have documented throughout, contrary to the position held by opponents of the BIE designation, there are indeed multiple common threads through various iterations of BIE that can be traced and understood along a historical continuum.

Following the abolition of slavery and through the Great Migration from South to North, black Americans struggled to understand the nature and role of their community within the United States while, at the same time, dealing with segregation, prejudice, and lack of equality before the law.

For some, that understanding required a rejection of an American identity as such and the adoption of an identity intended to set them apart from the rest of American society. That took on an ethnic dimension (in the case of Moorish Science), a racial/religious dimension (in the case of NOI), or a national/political dimension (in the case of adherents to Marxist black liberation doctrines). In each case there can be detected the tragic impact of foreign subversion, which exploited the challenges faced by the black community for the geopolitical ends of America's opponents. They included the pre-war efforts of the Imperial Japan's Black Dragon Society and the Soviets' scheme to establish a "Black Belt" homeland, to NOI's close ties to rogue states such as Iran and Libya, to Cuban support for black urban revolutionaries of both the 1960s and today.

We also see that, across the spectrum of BIE, groups continue to struggle with questions that have repeatedly troubled their predecessors. These include the role of charismatic and often corrupt leaders and how to handle succession, the role and purpose of taking up arms, the distinction between organized criminal activity for political purposes and for its own sake, the role of above-ground and underground groups, interacting in the broader political space without being forced to compromise, how to address foreign support, and whether to be hierarchically centralized or decentralized.

However strange the beliefs systems held by these BIE groups may appear to outsiders, in each case they are internally consistent systems that their adherents take seriously and on behalf of which some adherents are willing to engage in acts of violence and criminality. Because it is the duty of the police to uphold the system and the laws that some of these adherents reject and abhor, in many cases it is the police who are most aggressively targeted and bear the brunt of violence. But as we have documented, no groups are ultimately immune, including members of the black community itself, who are often victimized by such adherents for political or criminal reasons, particularly if they refuse to acquiesce to what these adherents view as the "correct" black identity.

What we should not do is engage in a kind of bigotry of low expectations, which treats the belief systems of BIEs as somehow less relevant, less worthy of study, or less of a threat than other ideologies, such as those held by jihadists or white supremacists. BIE adherents are not purely reactive and emotional victims at the mercy of the world around them. Within the history of BIE movements are highly trained and constantly adapting cadres with sophisticated doctrines, strategies, and tactics—and the professional capability to coordinate substantial acts of violence to achieve genuine political purposes.

Endnotes

1. FBI Counterterrorism Division, "Intelligence Assessment: Black Identity Extremists Likely Motivated to Target Law Enforcement Officers," August 3, 2017, https://www.documentcloud.org/documents/4067711-BIE-Redacted.html.

2. FBI Counterterrorism Division, "Intelligence Assessment."

3. Ned Parker and Mimi Dwyer, "Dallas Gunman Was Drawn to Anger of 'Black Power' Groups," Reuters, July 8, 2016, https://www.reuters.com/article/us-usa-police-blackmilitants/dallas-gunman-was-drawn-to-anger-of-black-power-groups-idUSKCN0ZP01M.

4. Priscilla DeGregory, Kevin Sheehan, and Kirstan Conley, "Black Panther Hails Ax Attack on Cops," *New York Post*, October 27, 2014, https://nypost.com/2014/10/27/new-black-panther-group-hails-ax-attacker/.

5. Bill Gertz, "Gavin Long, Cop Killer, Linked to Separatists," *Washington Times*, July 20, 2016, https://apnews.com/article/0324ed39921cfc-b1a1d17aff37328f63.

6. Jana Winters and Sharon Weinberger, "The FBI's New U.S. Terrorist Threat: 'Black Identity Extremists,'" *Foreign Policy*, October 6, 2017, https://foreignpolicy.com/2017/10/06/the-fbi-has-identified-a-new-domestic-terrorist-threat-and-its-black-identity-extremists/.

7. Ali Breland, "ACLU Wants FBI Records on Activists Labeled 'Black Identity Extremists,'" *The Hill*, October 18, 2017, https://thehill.com/policy/national-security/356016-aclu-files-request-for-fbi-to-release-surveillance-documents-of/.

8. Mike Gonzalez, *BLM: The Making of a Marxist Revolution* (New York: Encounter Books, 2021), 135.

9. Ari Melber and Diana Marinaccio, "Sharp Rise in Ambush Killings Leaves Police Officers, Families on Edge," NBC News, December 29, 2016, https://www.nbcnews.com/news/us-news/sharp-rise-ambush-killings-leaves-police-officers-families-edge-n700891.

10   Judith Weisenfeld, *New World A-Coming: Black Religion and Racial Identity during the Great Migration* (New York: New York University Press, 2016), 5.

11   Weisenfeld, 15.

12   J. Gordon Melton, "Nation of Islam," *Encyclopedia Britannica*, August 26, 2022, https://www.britannica.com/topic/Nation-of-Islam.

13   FBI, "Moorish Science Temple of America," Part 8, p. 1, http://vault.fbi.gov/Moorish%20Science%20Temple%20of%20America.

14   Toby Harnden, "Sect Inspired 'Leader of Sears Tower Plot,'" *The Telegraph*, June 25, 2006, https://web.archive.org/web/20110604012347/https://www.telegraph.co.uk/news/world-news/northamerica/usa/1522288/Sect-inspired-leader-of-Sears-Tower-plot.html.

15   Daniel Pipes, "A Century of Black American Islam," *Washington Times*, December 26, 2014, http://www.washingtontimes.com/news/2013/dec/26/pipes-a-century-of-black-american-islam/ .

16   Shaykh Ra Saadi El—Moorish Mahdi, "Rebuttal from Moorish Science Temple of America—1928," Danielpipes.org, January 13, 2014, http://www.danielpipes.org/13929/moorish-science-temple-rebuttal.

17   Prince Hall Grand Lodge, "A Brief History of Prince Hall Freemasonry in Massachusetts," https://www.princehall.org/african-lodge-459/.

18   "Noble Drew Ali," in *African American Lives*, ed. Henry Louis Gates and Evelyn Brooks Higgenbotham (Chicago: Oxford University Press US, 2004).

19   Saadi El, "Rebuttal."

20   Eddie S. Glaude Jr., *African American Religion* (Oxford: Oxford University Press, 1968), 104.

21   See, for example, Divine El-Bey YouTube channel at https://www.youtube.com/watch?v=vx1w2bfR9tk&list=UU35C7YeUN3OLjCEnOb-7T8uw.

22   FBI, "Moorish Science Temple of America," Part 2, p. 70.

23   Saadi El, "Rebuttal."

24   Glaude, *African American Religion*.

25 Edward Curtis, "African American Muslims," from "Encyclopedia of Muslim-American History" Facts on File, 2010, p. 13.

26 Thomas Peele, *Killing the Messenger* (New York: Crown Publishing, 2012), 48.

27 Susan Nance, "Respectability and Representation: The Moorish Science Temple, Morocco, and Black Public Culture in 1920s Chicago," *American Quarterly* 54, no. 4 (December 2002), http://muse.jhu.edu/journals/aq/summary/v054/54.4nance.html.

28 Noble Drew Ali, "Prophet Warns All Moslems—Governors Ordered to Read Proclamation at Each Meeting," Hermetic Library, January 15, 1929, http://hermetic.com/moorish/warning.html.

29 New York Public Library, "Archives of the Moorish American Science Temple 1926-1967," http://archives.nypl.org/scm/20888#overview.

30 Peele, *Killing the Messenger*, 53.

31 Sheikh Way-El, "Noble Drew Ali and The Moorish Science Temple of America: The Movement that Started it All" Moorish Science Temple of America, (2013), pg. 113

32 Peele, *Killing the Messenger*, 53-54.

33 Peele, *Killing the Messenger*, 55.

34 Fathi Ali Abdat, "The Sheiks of Sedition: Father Prophet Mohammed Bey, Mother Jesus Rosie Bey, and Kansas City's Moors (1933–1945)," *Journal of Religion and Violence* 3, no. 1 (2015): 7-34, https://www.jstor.org/stable/26671449.

35 Abdat, "The Sheiks of Sedition," 20.

36 Abdat, "The Sheiks of Sedition," 21.

37 FBI, "Moorish Science Temple of America," Part 2.

38 FBI, "Domestic Terrorism: The Sovereign Citizens Movement," April 10, 2010, http://www.fbi.gov/news/stories/2010/april/sovereigncitizens_041310.

39 MSTA, "Home Page," http://www.moorishsciencetempleofamericainc.com/.

40 "The Warning For Moors Who Are Confused On How To Navigate And The Need To Learn About the National Side Is Getting Louder And More Serious," Moorish American National Republic, October, 19, 2012 https://web.archive.org/web/20160813093403/https://moorishamericannationalrepublic.com/news/the-warning-for-moors-who-are-confused-on-how-to-navigate-the-national-side-and-the-need-to-get-it-together-is-getting-louder/.

41 See for example: Van Bailon Youtube Channel, "Moorish Sovereign Citizen Thinks Driving Without Plates is Legal | Illinois State Police Disagree," December 17, 2022, Youtube.com, https://www.youtube.com/watch?v=jWqdjNjePmU.

42 Dan Morse, "'Moorish American National' Charged with Trying to Take Mansion," *Washington Post*, March 18, 2013, http://www.washingtonpost.com/local/moorish-american-national-charged-with-trying-to-take-mansion/2013/03/18/b6d4524c-6ece-11e2-aa58-243de-81040ba_story.html.

43 Gustavo Valdes, "FBI: 'Sovereign Citizens' Fraudulently Taking Over Foreclosed Homes," CNN, March 9, 2011.

44 Cristin Severance and Hanna Merzbach, "Here's What the 'Sovereign Citizen' Defense Is, and How It's Linked to the Portland 'Red House,'" *KGW News*, December 10, 2020, https://www.kgw.com/article/news/local/sovereign-citizen-defense-did-not-work-in-saving-the-red-house-from-foreclosure-in-portland/283-80d4c5e1-1d02-4f53-968a-a323de8a99d2.

45 Nick Bundick, "Anti-Fascist, Sovereign Citizen Tactics Combine at Red House," *KOIN News*, December 16, 2020, https://www.koin.com/news/anti-fascist-sovereign-citizen-tactics-combine-at-red-house/.

46 Kyle Shideler, " Situation Report: Antifa Repels Police, Seizes Section of Portland Neighborhood, in 'Eviction Defense,'" Center for Security Policy, December 9, 2020, https://centerforsecuritypolicy.org/situation-report-antifa-repels-police-seizes-section-of-portland-neighborhood-in-eviction-defense/.

47 FBI, "Black Identity Extremists Likely Motivated to Target Law Enforcement Officers," August 3, 2017, https://docs.house.gov/meetings/JU/JU08/20210224/111227/HHRG-117-JU08-20210224-SD007.pdf.

48. *New Orleans Times-Picayune*, "Gavin Long Belonged to Washitaw Nation. Who Are They?," July 7, 2021, https://www.nola.com/news/crime_police/article_fd826206-6fd4-52b7-bf4e-3eaa07d93cbc.html.

49. *The Advocate*, "Read Suicide Note Left by Gavin Eugene Long, Gunman in Deadly Baton Rouge Officer Shooting in July 2016," June 30, 2017, https://www.theadvocate.com/baton_rouge/news/baton_rouge_officer_shooting/article_9748d2c0-5daa-11e7-af6d-ab3966e08d70.html.

50. *CBS Boston*, "I-Team: Jahmal Latimer Identified as Leader of Wakefield Standoff Suspects Called 'Rise of the Moors,'" July 3, 2021, https://www.cbsnews.com/boston/news/jahmal-latimer-rise-of-moors-moorish-american-arms-wakefield-standoff-i95/.

51. E. R. Ship, "Chicago Gang Sues to Be Recognized as Religion," *New York Times*, December 25, 1985, http://www.nytimes.com/1985/12/27/us/chicago-gang-sues-to-be-recognized-as-religion.html.

52. FBI, "The El Rukns," Part 2, http://vault.fbi.gov/el-rukn.

53. Ship, "Chicago Gang Sues to Be Recognized as Religion."

54. Maurice Possley, "Police Cracked Secret El Rukn Code," *Chicago Tribune*, December 14, 1986, http://articles.chicagotribune.com/1986-12-14/news/8604030327_1_el-rukns-jeff-fort-street-gang/2.

55. William Reckenwald, "Verdict May Break El Rukn," *Chicago Tribune*, October 23, 1988, http://articles.chicagotribune.com/1988-10-23/news/8802090493_1_el-rukn-rukn-leaders-jeff-fort.

56. Rudolph Unger, "Rukn Security Gets Stung," *Chicago Tribune*, June 20, 1986, http://articles.chicagotribune.com/1986-06-20/news/8602140198_1_el-rukn-jeff-fort-street-gangs.

57. Associated Press, "Jerry Lewis-Bey: Urban Savior or Drug Lord?," June 1, 1993, *The Telegraph*, http://news.google.com/newspapers?nid=2209&dat=19930601&id=gYJKAAAAIBAJ&sjid=zZMMAAAAIBAJ&pg=5619,16285.

58. Robert Snell, "Feds: Fez-Wearing Drug Dealers Deserve Life in Prison," *Detroit News*, October 14, 2014, http://www.detroitnews.com/story/news/local/wayne-county/2014/10/14/fez-detroit-drugs-kingpin-trial/17251727/.

59 Tresa Baldas, "Ex-Detroit Lawmaker Gets 1yr in Prison; Aided Drug Ring," *Detroit Free Press*, September 19, 2014, http://www.freep.com/story/news/local/michigan/detroit/2014/09/18/kenneth-daniels-sentenced/15855253/.

60 Toby Hardnen, "Sect Inspired 'Leader of Sears Tower Plot,'" *The Telegraph*, June 25, 2006, http://www.telegraph.co.uk/news/worldnews/northamerica/usa/1522288/Sect-inspired-leader-of-Sears-Tower-plot.html.

61 *BBC News*, "Sears Tower Bomb Plot Leader Narseal Batiste Jailed," November 20, 2009, http://news.bbc.co.uk/2/hi/8371671.stm.

62 Curtis, "African American Muslims," 13.

63 Carl Allen, "Suspicions in the Death of Malcolm X," *Buffalo News*, May 30, 1993, https://buffalonews.com/news/suspicions-in-the-death-of-malcolm-x/article_4a25e835-4c7d-5b73-bc9d-b30b4a2c0d05.html.

64 FBI, "Nation of Islam," Part 1, https://vault.fbi.gov/Nation%20of%20Islam/Nation%20of%20Islam%20Part%201%20of%203/view.

65 Peele, *Killing the Messenger*, 46-47.

66 Peele, *Killing the Messenger*, 54-56.

67 Peele, *Killing the Messenger*, 80-84.

68 Edward Curtis, "Nation of Islam," in *Handbook of Islamic Sects and Movements*, ed. Muhammad Afzal Upal and Carole M. Cusack (Leiden, The Netherlands: Brill, 2021), accessed at https://www.jstor.org/stable/10.1163/j.ctv1v7zbv8.d. 37.

69 Claude A. Clegg III, "Message from the Wilderness of North America: Elijah Muhammad and the Nation of Islam, c. 1960," *Journal for MultiMedia History* 1, no. 1 (Fall 1998), https://www.albany.edu/jmmh/vol1no1/elijahmuhammad.html.

70 Elijah Muhammad, "Lost Found Muslim Lesson No. 1," https://www.afrostyly.com/english/afro/diverse/120_lessons.htm#114.

71 ADL, "The Nation of Islam," September 1, 2021, https://www.adl.org/resources/profiles/the-nation-of-islam.

72 Elijah Muhammad, "Why They Urge You to Eat the Swine," in *How to Eat to Live*, https://www.farrakhanfactor.com/library/htetl1/htetl1_4.html.

73 Peele, *Killing the Messenger*, 97-98.

74 Alex Haley, "Alex Haley Interviews Malcolm X (May 1963)," *Playboy*, May 1963, https://alexhaley.com/2020/07/24/alex-haley-interviews-malcolm-x/.

75 Peele, *Killing the Messenger*, 99.

76 Peele, *Killing the Messenger*, 101-102.

77 Peele, *Killing the Messenger*, 103-106.

78 Malcolm X, "The Ballot or the Bullet," speech in Cleveland, OH, April 3, 1964, http://www.edchange.org/multicultural/speeches/malcolm_x_ballot.html.

79 Malcolm X, "The Ballot or the Bullet."

80 Malcolm X, "The Ballot or the Bullet."

81 Malcolm X, "The Ballot or the Bullet."

82 *New York Times*, "Malcolm X Splits with Muhammad: Suspended Muslim Leader Plans Black Nationalist Political Movement," March 9, 1964, https://archive.ph/LoanR#selection-319.0-319.98.

83 Smithsonian Channel, "Malcolm X's Explosive Comments About Elijah Muhammed," YouTube video, February 23, 2018, https://www.youtube.com/watch?v=pibigIqFkj8.

84 Sam McPheeters, "When Malcolm X Met the Nazis," *Vice*, April 15, 2015, https://www.vice.com/en/article/dpwamv/when-malcolm-x-met-the-nazis-0000620-v22n4; Malcolm X press conference, 1965, accessible at https://twitter.com/DumisaniTemsgen/status/1586673236418363392?s=20&t=aXicpIuorMDnsexJ8KJjpA.

85 John Mallon, "Malcolm X Home Firebombed," *New York Daily News*, February 15, 1965, https://www.nydailynews.com/news/crime/malcolm-x-home-firebombed-1965-article-1.2529655.

86 James Barron, "Making It Official: Verdict Overturned in Malcolm X Case," *New York Times*, November 19, 2021, https://archive.ph/P0sXj#selection-383.0-383.56.

87 FBI, "Five-Percenters," Part 1, p. 36, https://vault.fbi.gov/5percent/five-percenters-part-01-of-01/view.

88 Robert Tanner, "'Five Percent' Adherents Spread Faith—or Fantasy," *Los Angeles Times*, January 3, 1999, https://archive.ph/encwI.

89 Don Terry, "W. D. Muhammad: A Leap of Faith" *Hartford Courant*, October 20, 2002, https://archive.ph/8fLE.

90 Terry, "W. D. Muhammad."

91 Richard Lei, "Louis Farrakhan, Calypso Charmer," *Washington Post*, October 14, 1995, https://web.archive.org/web/20180220155307/https://www.washingtonpost.com/archive/lifestyle/1995/10/14/louis-farrakhan-calypso-charmer/40613502-02c1-48c0-8cde-8c0024d06015/.

92 *Chicago Tribune*, "Farrakhan Admits Role in Killing," May 10, 2000, https://web.archive.org/web/20200211170625/https://www.chicagotribune.com/news/ct-xpm-2000-05-10-0005110065-story.html.

93 Louis Farrakhan, "'The Wheel'—That Great Mother Plane: Allah's (God's) Calling Card," *The Final Call*, December 11, 2013, https://new.finalcall.com/2013/12/11/the-wheel-that-great-mother-plane-allahs-gods-calling-card.

94 Hebert McCann, "Farrakhan Delivers Insult While Denying He's Anti-Semitic," Associated Press, May 10, 2019, https://apnews.com/article/alex-jones-north-america-chicago-michael-pfleger-social-media-70da24ff7b344c098e91d9b3505a98e0; ADL, "Background: Louis Farrakhan in His Own Words," January 12, 2013, https://www.adl.org/education/resources/reports/nation-of-islam-farrakhan-in-his-own-words.

95 Debbie Wilgoren, "Farrakhan's Speech: Masons, Mysticism, and More," *Washington Post*, October 22, 1995, https://archive.ph/xY5k1.

96 Ricky Riley, "8 Facts about the First Million Man March in 1995 You May Not Know," *Atlanta Black Star*, October 21, 2015, https://atlantablackstar.com/2015/10/21/8-facts-about-the-first-million-man-march-in-1995-you-may-not-know/; see also Wikipedia, "Million Man March," https://en.wikipedia.org/wiki/Million_Man_March#Program.

97 Terry, "W. D. Muhammad."

98   ADL, "Federal Funds for NOI Security Firms: Financing Farrakhan's Ministry of Hate," 1998, https://web.archive.org/web/20121005145712/http://www.adl.org/issue_nation_of_islam/reports/financing.pdf.

99   Mary B. W. Tabor, "Muslim Guards: Security Unit Maintaining Pride," *New York Times*, January 6, 1992, https://www.nytimes.com/1992/01/06/nyregion/muslim-guards-security-unit-maintaining-pride.html.

100 ADL, "Federal Funds for NOI Security Firms," 8.

101 ADL, "Federal Funds for NOI Security Firms," 20.

102 Peele, *Killing the Messenger*, 132-133.

103 For more on Your Black Muslim Bakery and the Yusuf Ali Bey criminal enterprise, see the Chauncey Bailey project at https://chaunceybaileyproject.org/.

104 Sean Patrick Griffin, *Philadelphia's "Black Mafia:" A Social and Political History* (New York: Kluwer Academic Publishers, 2003), 18-25.

105 Sean Patrick Griffin, *Philadelphia's "Black Mafia:" A Social and Political History* (New York: Kluwer Academic Publishers, 2003), 18-25.

106 *New York Times*, "Muslim Aim Called 'to Maim and Kill' at Brooklyn Store," June 19, 1974, https://www.nytimes.com/1974/06/19/archives/muslim-aim-called-to-maim-and-kill-at-brooklyn-store.html.

107 Griffin, *Philadelphia's "Black Mafia,"* 38.

108 Eddie Mueller, "Zebra Murders Meant to Start Race War," *SFGate*, September 17, 2006, https://www.sfgate.com/books/article/Zebra-murders-meant-to-start-race-war-2469576.php.

109 Mueller, "Zebra Murders."

110 Mueller, "Zebra Murders."

111 Clark Howard in his book *Zebra* attributes more than 270 killings to the Death Angels throughout California, 45 of which he identifies as known to the state attorney general's office. Clark Howard, *Zebra* (New York: Richard Marek Publishers, 1979).

112 Nate Gartrell, "Last Two Living 'Zebra' Killers Denied Parole; Tied to Massive California Murder Spree Targeting Whites at Random," *San Jose Mercury News*, January 28, 2020, https://www.mercurynews.com/2020/01/28/last-two-living-zebra-killers-denied-parole-tied-to-massive-california-murder-spree-targeting-whites-at-random/.

113 Lee Romney, "'Zebra Killer' J. C. X. Simon Found Dead in San Quentin Prison Cell," *Los Angeles Times*, March 13, 2015, https://www.latimes.com/local/lanow/la-me-ln-zebra-killer-jcx-simon-dead-20150313-story.html.

114 Paul Danish, "Oklahoma Isn't the First to See Radicalist Beheadings," *Boulder Weekly*, October 16, 2014, https://boulderweekly.com/opinion/danish-plan/oklahoma-isnrsquot-the-first-to-see-radicalist-beheadings/.

115 Peele, *Killing the Messenger*, 76.

116 Julia Scheeres, "The Zebra Killers" The Crime Library, https://crimelibrary.org/notorious_murders/mass/zebra_murders/15.html.

117 Jason D. Antos, "Recognition for Cardillo After Four Decades," *Queens Gazette*, February 25, 2015, https://www.qgazette.com/articles/recognition-for-cardillo-after-four-decades/.

118 NYPD, "Report and Analysis of the Muslim Mosque Incident," 1973, p. 16, https://nypdhistory.com/wp-content/uploads/2017/03/19720414-Harlem-Mosque-Incident-Report-Analysis-copy.pdf.

119 Micah Morrison, "Did an FBI Call Accidentally Kill an NYPD Officer?," *New York Post*, April 19, 2015, https://nypost.com/2015/04/19/did-an-fbi-call-accidentally-kill-an-nypd-officer/.

120 Morrison, "Did an FBI Call Accidentally Kill an NYPD Officer?"

121 Morrison, "Did an FBI Call Accidentally Kill an NYPD Officer?"

122 NYPD, "Report and Analysis of the Muslim Mosque Incident."

123 George Goodman Jr., "Muslim Minister Assails Police Action," *New York Times*, April 16, 1972, https://www.nytimes.com/1972/04/16/archives/muslim-minister-assails-police-action.html.

124 NYPD, "Report and Analysis of the Muslim Mosque Incident."

125 Les Ledbetter, "Police Are Urged to Shift Whites," *New York Times*, May 1, 1972, https://www.nytimes.com/1972/05/01/archives/police-are-urged-to-shift-whites-5000-attend-rally-to-back-allblack.html.

126 Michael Knight, "Muslims Purge Police Members," *New York Times*, October 29, 1972, https://www.nytimes.com/1972/10/29/archives/muslims-purge-police-members-order-is-said-to-fear-they-were.html.

127 James Markham, "Murphy Defends Police Action at Harlem Mosque and Bans Transfer of White Policeman," *New York Times*, April 17, 1972, https://www.nytimes.com/1972/04/17/archives/murphy-defends-police-action-at-harlem-mosque-and-bars-transfer-of.html.

128 David Burnham, "Police Here List 'Sensitive' Spots; Mosque Cited," *New York Times*, May 14, 1972, https://www.nytimes.com/1972/05/14/archives/police-here-list-sensitive-spots-mosque-is-cited.html.

129 Richard Perez-Pena, "8 Police Officers Hurt in Clash at Harlem Mosque," *New York Times*, January 11, 1994, https://www.nytimes.com/1994/01/11/nyregion/8-police-officers-hurt-in-clash-at-harlem-mosque.html.

130 Michael Tomasky, "The Day Everything Changed," *New York Magazine*, September 22, 2008, https://nymag.com/anniversary/40th/50652/.

131 U.S. Department of State, *Libya's Continuing Responsibility for Terrorism*, November 1991, https://www.cia.gov/readingroom/docs/CIA-RDP96-00789R001001430004-9.pdf.

132 Edward D. Sargent, "$5 Million Qaddafi Loan to Go to Toiletry Firm," *Washington Post*, May 4, 1985, https://www.washingtonpost.com/archive/politics/1985/05/04/5-million-qaddafi-loan-to-go-to-toiletry-firm/cf68f65f-e71b-4dee-ae6b-f14f70f84706/.

133 Tom Heneghan, "Qaddafi's Secret Missionaries," Reuters, March 29, 2012, https://www.reuters.com/article/us-libya-missionary/special-report-gaddafis-secret-missionaries-idUSBRE82S07T20120329.

134 Sargent, "$5 Million Qaddafi Loan."

135 John Lancaster, "Gadhafi Sees Alliance with Farrakhan," *New York Times*, January 26, 1996, https://www.washingtonpost.com/archive/

politics/1996/01/26/gadhafi-sees-alliance-with-farrakhan/92192789-f888-425f-bf41-0b3780f81c9b/.

136 Richard Stevenson, "Officials to Block Qaddafi Gift to Farrakhan," *New York Times*, August 28, 1996, https://www.nytimes.com/1996/08/28/us/officials-to-block-qaddafi-gift-to-farrakhan.html.

137 Ryan Haggerty, "Farrakhan Condemns Killing of Libyan Leader Moammar Gadhafi," *Chicago Tribune*, October 25, 2011, https://www.chicagotribune.com/news/breaking/chi-farrakhan-condemns-killing-of-libyan-leader-moammar-gadhafi-20111025-story.html.

138 *Time Magazine*, "Gaddafi's Goons," December 7, 1987, https://content.time.com/time/subscriber/article/0,33009,966132,00.html.

139 Matt O'Connor, "Rukn Chieftain Says He Gave Cocaine to Aides of Farrakhan," *Chicago Tribune*, June 7, 1991.

140 ADL, "Federal Funds for NOI Security Firms," 30.

141 Tasmin News Agency, "Louis Farrakhan Leads 'Death to America' Slogan in Iran," November 5, 2018, https://www.tasnimnews.com/en/news/2018/11/05/1869419/louis-farrakhan-leads-death-to-america-slogan-in-iran-video.

142 ADL, "Federal Funds for NOI Security Firms," 30.

143 Emily Davies, Justin Jouvenal, and Michael E. Miller, "Family and Friends Concerned Noah Green Was Unraveling Before Capitol Attack," *Washington Post*, April 2, 2021, https://www.washingtonpost.com/local/public-safety/noah-green-capitol-attack/2021/04/02/74f75802-93fe-11eb-a74e-1f4cf89fd948_story.html.

144 Davies, Jouvenal, and Miller, "Family and Friends Concerned."

145 Davies, Jouvenal, and Miller, "Family and Friends Concerned."

146 Lee Brown, "Nation of Islam Mourns 'Brother' Noah Green Who Died While Killing Capitol Cop," *New York Post*, April 7, 2021, https://nypost.com/2021/04/07/nation-of-islam-mourns-noah-green-who-died-killing-capitol-cop/.

147 Kyle Shideler, "FBI Alleges Black Identity Extremist Groups Were Acting as 'Instruments of the Russian Government,'" Center for Security Policy, August 4, 2022, https://centerforsecuritypolicy.org/fbi-alleges-

148. Shideler, "FBI Alleges Black Identity Extremist Groups."

149. Michal Wojnowski, "Racial Conflicts Created by the Russian Security Authorities in the USA," Warsaw Institute, February 2022, p. 14, https://warsawinstitute.org/wp-content/uploads/2022/02/RS_01-2022_EN.pdf.

150. Wojnowski, 16.

151. Robert Greene II, "A Southern Vanguard: The Lost History of Southern Communism," *The Nation*, June 1, 2020, https://www.thenation.com/article/politics/red-black-white-alabama-communist-party-mary-stanton/; "Elaine Massacre of 1919," in *CALS Encyclopedia of Arkansas*, https://encyclopediaofarkansas.net/entries/elaine-massacre-of-1919-1102/.

152. African Blood Brotherhood, "Program of the African Blood Brotherhood," 1922, from *Black Revolutionaries in the United States,* Communist Research Center, 2016, pg. 44, https://files.libcom.org/files/crc_ci_vol_two_0_1_0.pdf.

153. H. M. Wicks, former member of the Central Executive Committee of the CPUSA, *Eclipse of October* (Chicago: Challenge Publishers), p. 249, as cited in *The Revival of the Communist International and Its Significance for the United States*, Staff Study by the Subcommittee to Investigate the Administration of the Internal Security Act and Other Internal Security Laws, Committee on the Judiciary, U.S. Senate, 86th Congress, First Session, 1959, p. 27.

154. Gonzalez, *BLM*, 33.

155. Gonzalez, *BLM*, 34.

156. FBI, "The Communist Party and the Negro: 1953-1956," October 1956, p. ii, https://www.eisenhowerlibrary.gov/sites/default/files/research/online-documents/civil-rights-eisenhower-administration/1956-10-communist-party-and-the-negro.pdf.

157. National Public Radio, "How 'Communism' Brought Racial Equality to the South," February 16, 2010, https://www.npr.org/templates/story/story.php?storyId=123771194.

158. FBI, "The Communist Party and the Negro," p. iii.

159 Karen Dubinsky, "Cuba and the Making of a United States Left," Black Perspectives, September 14, 2018, https://www.aaihs.org/cuba-and-the-making-of-a-united-states-left/.

160 Robert Greene II, "The Civil Rights Movement Was Radical to Its Core," *Jacobin*, August 28, 2022, https://jacobin.com/2022/08/long-civil-rights-movement-communist-radical-roots.

161 Peter Collier and David Horowitz, *Destructive Generation* (New York: Encounter Books, 1989), 158-159.

162 Marvin X. Jackmon, "In Memoriam: Notes on Oakland Afro American Association Founder, Attorney Donald Warden, aka Khalid Abdullah Tariq al Mansour, Mentor of the Black Panthers," Black Bird Press News, August 19, 2018, https://blackbirdpressnews.blogspot.com/2018/08/in-memoriam-notes-on-oakland-afro.html.

163 Reelblack One, "Burn Baby, Burn—The Uncensored Version of The Los Angeles Riots (1965) | Donald Warden Johnny Nash," YouTube video, April 18, 2021, https://www.youtube.com/watch?v=sgB2QQ1fQjE.

164 Jackmon, "In Memoriam."

165 Collier and Horowitz, *Destructive Generation*, 159.

166 Ann Coulter, "Negroes with Guns," AnneCoulter.com, April 18, 2012, https://anncoulter.com/2012/04/18/negroes-with-guns/.

167 Maxwell Stanford, "Revolutionary Action Movement (RAM): A Case Study of an Urban Revolutionary Movement in Western Capitalist Society," Atlanta University, May, 1968, p. 58, https://www.freedomarchives.org/Documents/Finder/Black%20Liberation%20Disk/Black%20Power!/SugahData/Dissertations/Stanford.S.pdf.

168 David Stout, "Robert F. Williams, 71, Civil Rights Leader and Revolutionary," *New York Times*, October 19, 1996, https://www.nytimes.com/1996/10/19/us/robert-f-williams-71-civil-rights-leader-and-revolutionary.html.

169 Kathleen Cleaver and Mabel Williams, "Self Respect, Self-Defense and Self Determination: A Presentation," in *Setting Sights: Histories and Reflections on Community Armed Self-Defense*, ed. Scott Crow (Oakland: PM Press, 2018), 147.

170 Darren Salter, "Robert F. Williams," Blackpast.com, December 9,

2007, https://www.blackpast.org/african-american-history/williams-robert-f-1925-1996/.

171 John Jones, "A History of the Revolutionary Action Movement" (master's thesis, George Washington University, 2019), 6.

172 "12-Point Program of the Revolutionary Action Movement (RAM)," 1964, https://abolitionnotes.org/ram/12point-program.

173 Stanford, "Revolutionary Action Movement," 99.

174 Stanford, "Revolutionary Action Movement," 87.

175 Stanford, "Revolutionary Action Movement," 102-103.

176 Stanford, "Revolutionary Action Movement," 122; Donna March, "Watts, Lowndes County, Oakland: The Founding of the Black Panther Party for Self Defense," Verso Books, October 14, 2016, https://www.versobooks.com/blogs/2882-watts-lowndes-county-oakland-the-founding-of-the-black-panther-party-for-self-defense.

177 SNCC Digital Gateway, "April 1960: Founding of the SNCC," https://snccdigital.org/events/founding-of-sncc/.

178 SNCC Digital Gateway, "Mississippi Freedom Democratic Party (MFDP)," https://snccdigital.org/inside-sncc/alliances-relationships/mfdp/.

179 James DeVinney, "Interview with John Hulett," from *Eyes on the Prize II: America at the Racial Crossroads 1965 to 1985,* Blackside Inc., October 18, 1988, http://repository.wustl.edu/concern/videos/jd4731438

180 DeVinney, "Interview with John Hulett."

181 Ethan Scott Barnett, "Stokely Carmichael: The Boy Before Black Power," Gotham Center, December 5, 2019, https://www.gothamcenter.org/blog/stokelycarmichael.

182 Martin Luther King Jr. Research and Education Institute, "Carmichael, Stokely," https://kinginstitute.stanford.edu/encyclopedia/carmichael-stokely.

183 Martin Luther King Jr. Research and Education Institute, "Carmichael, Stokely."

184 History Matters, "'We Must Destroy the Capitalistic System Which

Enslaves Us:' Stokely Carmichael Advocates Black Revolution," https://historymatters.gmu.edu/d/6461/.

185 DeVinney, "Interview with John Hulett."

186 The Sixties Project, "Student Nonviolent Coordinating Committee Position Paper: The Basis of Black Power," http://www2.iath.virginia.edu/sixties/HTML_docs/Resources/Primary/Manifestos/SNCC_black_power.html.

187 *Time Magazine*, "Atlanta: Stokely's Spark," September 16, 1966, https://content.time.com/time/subscriber/article/0,33009,836360,00.html.

188 Bill Carey, "A Vanderbilt Guest Starts a Riot," *Nashville Post*, April 3, 2008, https://www.nashvillepost.com/business/education/a-vanderbilt-guest-starts-a-riot/article_f0999458-e491-529b-aed9-0545123eff39.html.

189 "Riots, Civil and Criminal Disorders," *Hearings Before the Permanent Subcommittee on Investigations of the Committee on Government Operations*, U.S. Senate, 90th Congress, 1st session, November 1-6, 1967, pp. 145-185.

190 FBI, "Stokely Carmichael," Part 1, pp. 31-36, https://vault.fbi.gov/Stokely%20Carmichael/Stokely%20Carmichael%20Part%201%20of%205/view.

191 *Tampa Bay Times*, "K. Ture, Formerly Stokely Carmichael, Dies at 57," November 16, 1998, https://www.tampabay.com/archive/1998/11/16/k-ture-former-stokely-carmichael-dies-at-57/.

192 Bryan Burrough, *Days of Rage* (New York: Penguin Books, 2016), 47-48.

193 Andrea King Collier, "The Black Panthers: Revolutionaries, Free Breakfast Pioneers," *National Geographic*, November 4, 2015, https://www.nationalgeographic.com/culture/article/the-black-panthers-revolutionaries-free-breakfast-pioneers.

194 Huey P. Newton, "The Correct Handling of a Revolution," 1967, from *Black Revolutionaries in the United States,* Communist Research Center, 2016, https://files.libcom.org/files/crc_ci_vol_two_0_1_0.pdf, pg. 242

195 Fred Hampton, "Power Anywhere there's people," 1969, from *Black*

      Revolutionaries in the United States, Communist Research Center, 2016, https://files.libcom.org/files/crc_ci_vol_two_0_1_0.pdf pg. 247

196 *Sacramento Bee,* "Armed Black Panthers Invade Capitol," May 2, 1967, https://www.sacbee.com/news/local/history/article148667224.html.

197 Don McGaffin, "Arrest of Huey P. Newton and Bobby Seale," Bay Area Television Archive, May 3, 1967 https://diva.sfsu.edu/collections/sfbatv/bundles/206879.

198 The Sixties Project, "Rules of the Black Panther Party," http://www2.iath.virginia.edu/sixties/HTML_docs/Resources/Primary/Manifestos/Panther_rules.html.

199 Burrough, *Days of Rage,* 45.

200 Eldridge Cleaver, "On Ideology" 1969, from *Black Revolutionaries in the United States,* Communist Research Center, 2016, https://files.libcom.org/files/crc_ci_vol_two_0_1_0.pdf, pg. 247

201 Safiya Bukhari, "An Interview with Donald Cox, Former Black Panther Field Marshal," Safiya Bukhari-Ablbert Nuh Washington Foundation, March 31, 1992.

202 Collier and Horowitz, *Destructive Generation,* 162.

203 Burrough, *Days of Rage,* 47.

204 Kate Coleman, "Souled Out," *New West,* May 19, 1980, https://web.archive.org/web/20090326111123/http://colemantruth.net/kate1.pdf.

205 Burrough, *Days of Rage,* 185.

206 Don Cox, "An Insider's Take on How the Black Panther Party Was Hurt by Its Own Ideals," *Time,* February 13, 2019, https://time.com/5527603/don-cox-black-panther-party/.

207 Michael Moynihan, "Whitewashing the Panthers," *Daily Beast,* July 12, 2017, https://www.thedailybeast.com/whitewashing-the-black-panthers.

208 *New York Times,* "Panther Killing Is Laid to 'Purge,'" April 16, 1971, https://www.nytimes.com/1971/04/16/archives/panther-killing-is-laid-to-purge-kimbro-is-unshaken-in-his.html.

209   Paul Bass, "Black Panther Torture 'Trial' Tape Surfaces," *New Haven Independent*, February 21, 2013, https://www.newhavenindependent.org/index.php/article/rackley_trial_tape_surfaces/.

210   Collier and Horowitz, *Destructive Generation*, 313.

211   *Desert Sun*, "Execution of Panther Discovered," April 21, 1971, https://cdnc.ucr.edu/?a=d&d=DS19710421&.

212   Huey P. Newton, "On The Defection of Eldridge Cleaver from the Black Panther Party and the Defection of the Black Panther Party From the Black Community" from *Black Revolutionaries in the United States,* Communist Research Center, 2016, pg. 256

213   Collier and Horowitz, *Destructive Generation*, 167.

214   Collier and Horowitz, *Destructive Generation*, 167.

215   Kate Coleman, "Just a Pack of Predators," *Los Angeles Times*, June 22, 2003, https://www.latimes.com/archives/la-xpm-2003-jun-22-op-coleman22-story.html.

216   Coleman, "Just a Pack of Predators."

217   Jennifer McNulty, "Police Arrest Suspect in Newton Killing," AP News, August 26, 1989, https://apnews.com/article/42c665d86b3dbf608e-38f45aae34c1f6.

218   Wallace Turner, "Panther Is Linked to Jail Break Gun," *New York Times*, August 28, 1971, https://www.nytimes.com/1971/08/28/archives/panther-is-linked-to-jail-break-gun-san-quentin-officials-trace.html.

219   Youcef Oussama Bounab, "Algeria's Forgotten Revolutionary History," *Africa Is a Country*, March 19, 2020, https://africasacountry.com/2020/03/algerias-forgotten-revolutionary-history/.

220   Bounab, "Algeria's Forgotten Revolutionary History."

221   Jaime Suchlicki and Eugene Pons, "Cuba's Commitment to Violence, Terrorism, and Anti-Americanism," Cuban Studies Institute, May 2020, https://cubanstudiesinstitute.us/principal/cubas-commitment-to-violence-terrorism-and-anti-americanism/.

222   Bounab, "Algeria's Forgotten Revolutionary History."

223   Daniel Swanson, "Cleaver Pronounces Panther Party Dead," *Harvard*

Crimson, November 1, 1971, https://www.thecrimson.com/article/1971/11/1/cleaver-pronounces-panther-party-dead-pthe/.

224 *Bablyon*, "Algeria," December 15, 1971, https://washingtonspark.files.wordpress.com/2020/05/1971-12-15-babylon-vol-1-no-3.pdf.

225 The Sixties Project, "Rules of the Black Panther Party."

226 Burrough, *Days of Rage*, 194.

227 Burrough, *Days of Rage*, 217.

228 Anonymous, "Revolutionary Armed Struggle," Abraham Guillen Press, August 2002, https://archive.org/details/RevolutionaryArmed-Struggle

229 Burrough, *Days of Rage*, 180.

230 Stanford, "Revolutionary Action Movement," 121.

231 Burrough, *Days of Rage*, 181.

232 *Frontline*, "Interview with Kathleen Cleaver," Spring 1997, https://www.pbs.org/wgbh/pages/frontline/shows/race/interviews/kcleaver.html.

233 Thomas J. Deakin, "The Legacy of Carlos Marighela," *FBI Law Enforcement Bulletin*, October 1974, p. 23.

234 Deakin, "The Legacy of Carlos Marighela," 22.

235 Deakin, "The Legacy of Carlos Marighela," 23.

236 Carlos Marighela, *Minimanual of the Urban Guerrilla* (1969, repr., Utrecht: Foreign Language Press, 2016), 75.

237 Caio Barretto Briso, "His Struggle Is Ours: Biopic of Slain 60s Rebel Hailed in Brazil with Anti-Bolsonaro Chants," *The Guardian*, December 10, 2021, https://www.theguardian.com/world/2021/dec/10/carlos-Marighela-film-brazil-jair-bolsonaro.

238 Burrough, *Days of Rage*, 176.

239 Conor Tomas Reed, "Assata Shakur: Always Welcome," *Left Voice*, July 11, 2017, https://www.leftvoice.org/assata-shakur-always-welcome/.

240 Burrough, *Days of Rage*, 239.

241 Amber Randall, "Meet the Cop-Killing Terrorist the Women's March

Is Bent on Honoring," *Daily Caller*, July 19, 2017 https://dailycaller.com/2017/07/19/meet-the-cop-killing-terrorist-the-womens-march-is-bent-on-honoring/.

242 Reed, "Assata Shakur: Always Welcome."

243 Katherine Hignett, "Who Is Assata Shakur? Backlash After Conference with 2020 Dems Starts with Words of Activist and Convicted Killer," *Newsweek*, April 3, 2019, https://www.newsweek.com/assata-shakur-black-power-activism-2020-elections-democrats-1384510.

244 CNN News, "He Was a Symbol': Eldridge Cleaver Dies at 62," May 1, 1998, http://www.cnn.com/US/9805/01/cleaver.late.obit/.

245 People's Response Team, "Cop-Watch 101," March 2017, https://web.archive.org/web/20180729075707/http://www.peoplesresponseteam-chicago.org/uploads/8/7/9/8/87981704/cop_watch_101_.pdf.

246 Berkeley Copwatch, "About," https://www.berkeleycopwatch.org/about.

247 People's Response Team, "Cop-Watch 101."

248 Jocelyn Simonson, "Copwatching," *California Law Review*, Quarter 4 (2016), https://brooklynworks.brooklaw.edu/cgi/viewcontent.cgi?article=1918&context=faculty.

249 Burrough, *Days of Rage*, 44.

250 See, for example, Ines Novacic, "As Groups Police the Police, Some Add Guns to the Mix," CBS News, January 22, 2015, https://www.cbsnews.com/news/policing-the-police-and-adding-guns-into-the-mix/.

251 Huey P. Newton Gun Club, "Local Objectives," https://hueypnewtongunclub.org/about. Emphasis added.

252 Huey P. Newton Gun Club, "Laws & Ethics," https://hueypnewtongunclub.org/laws-and-ethics.

253 Rocco Parascandola and Thomas Tracy, "NYPD Commissioner Bill Bratton Criticizes 'Epidemic' of Citizens Recording Arrests amid Backlash over Harlem Cop Caught Punching Man Who Filmed Him," *New York Daily News*, May 25, 2016, archived at: https://archive.is/rh45a#selection-1531.0-1531.148.

254 Burrough, *Days of Rage*; Kyle Shideler, ed., *Unmasking Antifa: Five*

Perspectives on a Growing Threat (Washington: Center for Security Policy Press, 2018), 47.

255   Erin Smith, "The tactics of Antifa," from *Unmasking Antifa: Five Perspectives on a Growing Threat* (Washington: Center for Security Policy Press, 2018), pg71

256   Scott Crow, "Defense in Dallas in the Twenty-First Century," in *Setting Sights*, 269.

257   Aaron Lake Smith, "Huey P. Newton Gun Club in Dallas Are Responding to Police Brutality with Armed Community Patrols," *Vice*, January 5, 2015, https://www.vice.com/en/article/5gk85a/huey-does-dallas-0000552-v22n1.

258   Crow, "Defense in Dallas in the Twenty-First Century," 270.

259   Graeme Wood, "A Black Army Rises to Fight the Racist Right," *The Atlantic*, April 2, 2021, https://www.theatlantic.com/politics/archive/2021/04/the-many-lives-of-grandmaster-jay/618408/.

260   Burrough, *Days of Rage*, 50.

261   Officer Down Memorial Page, "Officer Thomas E. Johnson," https://www.odmp.org/officer/7195-officer-thomas-e-johnson.

262   William Rosenau, "'Our Backs Are Against the Wall:' The Black Liberation Army and Domestic Terrorism in 1970s America," Studies in Conflict and Terrorism 36, no. 2 (2013), 176-192.

263   Adrian Alan, "Meet the Police Officers Murdered by the Black Panthers," Professional Gunfighter Blog, February 10, 2016, https://web.archive.org/web/20200718075651/https://progunfighter.com/murdered-by-the-black-panthers/.

264   Mike Wood, "Police History: The Black Panthers and the Rise of Anti-Cop Violence," *Police1*, November 13, 2015, https://www.police1.com/patrol-issues/articles/police-history-the-black-panthers-and-the-rise-of-anti-cop-violence-AWBENGibWIm08xmy/.

265   Burrough, *Days of Rage*, 49.

266   Collier and Horowitz, *Destructive Generation*, 168.

267   Canady v. State, 461 S.W.2d 53 (Tenn. Crim. App. 1970), Court of Criminal Appeals of Tennessee, https://www.courtlistener.com/opinion/1754293/canady-v-state/.

268 Burrough, *Days of Rage*, 196-207.

269 Burrough, *Days of Rage*, 215.

270 Officer Down Memorial Page, "Lieutenant Ted Cephus Elmore," https://www.odmp.org/officer/18721-lieutenant-ted-cephus-elmore.

271 Morris Kaplan, "9 Allegedly in Black Army Indicted Here," *New York Times*, August 24, 1973, https://www.nytimes.com/1973/08/24/archives/9-allegedly-in-black-army-indicted-here-9-allegedly-in-black.html.

272 Burrough, *Days of Rage*, 217.

273 Nick Breul and Desiree Luongo, *Making It Safer: A Study of Law Enforcement Fatalities Between 2010-2016*, DOJ, December 2017, p. 39, https://cops.usdoj.gov/RIC/Publications/cops-w0858-pub.pdf.

274 John Lott, "Ferguson Fake-Out: Justice Department's Bogus Report," *New York Post*, March 9, 2015, https://nypost.com/2015/03/09/ferguson-fake-out-justice-departments-bogus-report/.

275 Eric Westervelt, "Cities Looking to Reform Police Traffic Stops to Combat 'Fishing Expeditions,'" National Public Radio, April 16, 2021, https://www.npr.org/2021/04/16/988200868/cities-looking-to-reform-police-traffic-stops-to-combat-fishing-expeditions; Akhi Johnson and Erica Bryant, "End Police Stops for Minor Infractions," Vera Institute, October 4, 2021, https://www.vera.org/news/end-police-stops-for-minor-infractions.

276 Susannah N. Tapp and Elizabeth J. Davis, "*Contacts Between Police and the Public, 2020*," DOJ, November 2022, https://bjs.ojp.gov/sites/g/files/xyckuh236/files/media/document/cbpp20.pdf.

277 Joel F. Shults, "Anatomy of an Ambush," National Police Association, September 18, 2022, https://nationalpolice.org/anatomy-of-an-ambush/; Emily Zantow, "Ambush Attacks on Police up 139%, Report Finds," *Washington Times*, November 1, 2021, https://www.washingtontimes.com/news/2021/nov/1/ambush-attacks-police-139-report-finds/.

278 Shults, "Anatomy of an Ambush."

279 Burrough, *Days of Rage*, 75.

280 Joseph P. Fried, "2 Patrolmen Slain by Shots in Back; 2 Men Sought,"

New York Times, May 22, 1971, https://timesmachine.nytimes.com/timesmachine/1971/05/22/81943290.pdf.

281   Burrough, *Days of Rage*, 176.

282   Fried, "2 Patrolmen Slain."

283   For more on the history of the May 19th Communist Organization and Antifa see *Unmasking Antifa*; and Kyle Shideler, "The Real History of Antifa," *American Mind*, May 3, 2020, https://americanmind.org/salvo/the-real-history-of-antifa/.

284   Burrough, *Days of Rage*, 192.

285   John Koopman, "2nd Guilty Plea in 1971 Killing of S.F. Officer," *SFGate*, July 7, 2009, https://www.sfgate.com/bayarea/article/2nd-guilty-plea-in-1971-killing-of-S-F-officer-3226167.php.

286   Amber Randall, "Two Arrested After Trying to Start 'Race War' with 'Bomb' at Elementary School," Daily Caller, November 16, 2016, https://dailycaller.com/2016/11/24/two-arrested-after-trying-to-start-race-war-with-bomb-at-elementary-school/.

287   Ivana Hrynkiw, "Four Arrested, Charged with Attempting to Rob Trussville Bank and Creating Fake Bomb," *Birmingham Real-Time News*, February 13, 2017, https://www.al.com/news/birmingham/2017/02/four_arrested_charged_with_att.html.

288   Chuck Hustmyre, "Mark Essex, the Howard Johnson Sniper," *Crime Library*, https://www.crimelibrary.org/notorious_murders/mass/mark_essex/index.html.

289   Ron Franscell, "45 Years Ago Today, Mark Essex Unleashed Himself," RonFranscell.com, https://ronfranscell.com/2018/01/07/essex/.

290   Hustmyre, "Mark Essex."

291   Denise Noe, "Sniper Mark Essex," *Crime Magazine*, July 11, 2011, https://www.crimemagazine.com/sniper-mark-essex.

292   Associated Press, "Dallas Sniper Profile: Micah Johnson Was Sent Home from Afghanistan," July 9, 2016, https://www.theguardian.com/us-news/2016/jul/09/dallas-shooting-more-details-emerge-about-micah-xavier-johnson.

293   Avi Selk, Hannah Wise, and Conor Shine, "Eight Hours of Terror: How a Peaceful Protest Turned into the Dallas Police's Deadliest Day,"

Dallas Morning News, July 8, 2016, https://interactives.dallasnews.com/2016/dallas-police-ambush-timeline/.

294 Tanya Eiserer and Jason Trahan, "'We're in a Kill Zone:' Exclusive New Video Shows Deadly Dallas Ambush 5 Years Later," WFAA, July 7, 2021, https://www.wfaa.com/article/news/local/7-7/exclusive-new-video-deadly-dallas-ambush-july-7-2016-5-years-later/287-e69d3768-153f-4d3e-bc12-0f14c5f267f7.

295 Selk, Wise, and Shine, "Eight Hours of Terror."

296 Aaron Klein, "New Black Panther Leader: Cop Killer Micah Johnson 'Just Got Five of the Bastards,'" Breitbart.com, July 10, 2016, https://www.breitbart.com/middle-east/2016/07/10/exclusive-new-black-panther-leader-cop-killer-mica-johnson-just-got-five-bastards/.

297 DOJ and International Association of Chiefs of Police, *Ambush Attacks: A Risk Reduction Manual for Police*, 1974, https://www.ojp.gov/pdffiles1/Digitization/30021NCJRS.pdf.

298 Burrough, *Days of Rage*, 204.

299 Priscilla DeGregory, Kevin Sheehan, and Kirstan Conley, "Black Panther Hails Ax Attack on Cops," *New York Post*, October 27, 2014, https://nypost.com/2014/10/27/new-black-panther-group-hails-ax-attacker/.

300 Screenshots of Thompson's social media account are in possession of the author.

301 DOJ, "Eleven Members/Associates of Ummah Charged with Federal Violations," press release, October 28, 2009, https://archives.fbi.gov/archives/detroit/press-releases/2009/de102809.htm.

302 Justin Fenton, "Killer of 2 NYPD Officers First Shot Ex-Girlfriend in Owings Mills," *Baltimore Sun*, December 20, 2014, https://web.archive.org/web/20141221100903/http://www.baltimoresun.com/news/maryland/bs-md-co-owings-mills-shooting-20141220-story.html#page=1.

303 CBS Baltimore, "Police Connect Local Shooting to NYPD Officers' Killings," December 21, 2014, https://www.cbsnews.com/baltimore/news/police-connect-local-shooting-to-nypd-officers-murders/.

304 Larry Celona et al., "Gunman Executes 2 NYPD Cops in Garner

'Revenge,'" *New York Post*, December 20, 2014, https://nypost.com/2014/12/20/2-nypd-cops-shot-execution-style-in-brooklyn/.

305 Tina Moore and Bill Hutchinson, "Police Believe New York City Cop Killer Was a Member of the Black Guerrilla Family: Sources," *New York Daily News*, December 20, 2014, https://web.archive.org/web/20150109013542/https://www.nydailynews.com/news/national/killer-nypd-slays-ran-black-guerrilla-family-article-1.2052069.

306 Fenton, "Killer of 2 NYPD Officers."

307 Patrick Poole, "Did Cop Killer Ishmael Brinsley Visit Terror-Tied Brooklyn Mosque?," *PJ Media*, December 20, 2014, https://pjmedia.com/tatler/2014/12/20/did-cop-killer-ishmael-brinsley-visit-terror-tied-brooklyn-mosque-n197507.

308 FBI, "Robert Steele Collier," https://vault.fbi.gov/robert-steele-collier/Robert%20Steele%20Collier%20Part%2001%20of%2001/view.

309 FBI, "Robert Steele Collier."

310 Time Magazine, "New York: The Monumental Plot," February 26, 1965, https://content.time.com/time/subscriber/article/0,33009,833472-1,00.html.

311 David Fontaine Mitchell, "The Monumental Plot: An Overview of the Conspiracy to Destroy the Statue of Liberty, Liberty Bell, and Washington Monument," *Journal of Counterterrorism and Homeland Security International* 16, no. 4 (Winter 2010), p. 30, https://web.archive.org/web/20210812024611/http://www.davidfmitchell.com/uploads/4/3/4/0/43400967/the_monumental_plot_by_david_f._mitchell.pdf.

312 Mitchell, "The Monumental Plot," 34.

313 Mitchell, "The Monumental Plot," 34.

314 Morris Kaplan, "Bomb Plot is Laid to 21 Panthers," *New York Times*, April 3, 1969, https://timesmachine.nytimes.com/timesmachine/1969/04/03/90083782.html?pageNumber=36.

315 Edith Evans Asbury, "Black Panther Party Members Freed After Being Cleared of Charges," *New York Times*, May 14, 1971, https://www.nytimes.com/1971/05/14/archives/black-panther-party-members-freed-after-being-cleared-of-charges-13.html.

316 Kaplan, "Bomb Plot Laid to 21 Panthers." https://timesmachine.nytimes.com/timesmachine/1969/04/03/90083782.html?pageNumber=36.

317 Tom Wolfe, "Radical Chic: That Party at Lenny's," *New York Magazine*, June 8, 1970, https://nymag.com/news/features/46170/.

318 Asbury, "Black Panther Party Members Freed."

319 Robert Patrick, "Two Admit Plot to Blow Up Police Station, St. Louis County Prosecutor and Ferguson Police Chief," *St. Louis Post-Dispatch*, June 2, 2015, https://web.archive.org/web/20200902205726/https://www.stltoday.com/news/local/crime-and-courts/two-admit-plot-to-blow-up-police-station-st-louis-county-prosecutor-and-ferguson-police/article_47bc72ff-ad16-5ce7-b7be-432180fa555e.html.

320 Patrick, "Two Admit Plot."

321 DOJ, "Two Local Men Sentenced on Federal Explosives and Weapons Charges," press release, September 3, 2015, https://www.justice.gov/usao-edmo/pr/two-local-men-sentenced-federal-explosives-and-weapons-charges.

322 Justin Glawe, "The Black Panther Bomb Plot in St. Louis That Wasn't," *Daily Beast*, updated April 14, 2017, https://www.thedailybeast.com/the-black-panther-bomb-plot-in-st-louis-that-wasnt.

323 Kenya Vaughn, "Olajuwon's Next Act: Formerly Incarcerated Ferguson Activist Finds Purpose on Stage," *St. Louis American*, September 15, 2022, https://www.stlamerican.com/arts_and_entertainment/living_it/olajuwon-s-next-act/article_587e4c6e-3482-11ed-9f3a-a789c24ae85f.html.

324 FBI, "Robert Steele Collier."

325 Danny Wicentowski, "Targeted in a Ferguson FBI Sting, Olajuwon Davis Eyes His Next Act," *Riverfront Times*, August 4, 2021, https://www.riverfronttimes.com/news/targeted-in-a-ferguson-fbi-sting-olajuwon-davis-eyes-his-next-act-36007525.

326 United States v. Lorenzo Edward Ervin, Jr., 436 F.2d 1331 (5th Cir. 1971), https://www.courtlistener.com/opinion/294301/united-states-v-lorenzo-edward-ervin-jr/. See also an interview with Ervin at https://libcom.org/article/interview-lorenzo-komboa-ervin-1995.

327 Douglas Perry, "How Coos Bay's 'All-American Girl' Became a Daring

Skyjacker, Then Disappeared into 1970s Underground," *The Oregonian*, September 16, 2019, https://www.oregonlive.com/history/2019/09/how-coos-bays-all-american-girl-became-a-daring-skyjacker-then-disappeared-into-1970s-underground.html.

328 *Time Magazine*, "Algeria: Panthers on Ice," September 4, 1972, https://web.archive.org/web/20101022193351/http://www.time.com/time/magazine/article/0,9171,910394,00.html.

329 Tim Lister, "On the Run for 41 Years, Hijacker Traced to Portugal," CNN, September 28, 2011, https://www.cnn.com/2011/09/27/justice/hijacker-found/.

330 FBI, "Most Wanted: Domestic Terrorism," https://www.fbi.gov/wanted/dt.

331 The Kuwasi Balagoon Liberation School, "Orientation Power Point", Revolutionary Abolitionist Movement, N.D.

332 Associated Press, "Defendant Guilty in 2d Brink's Case," October 24, 1984, https://www.nytimes.com/1984/10/24/nyregion/the-city-defendant-guilty-in-2d-brink-s-case.html.

333 Russell Maroon Shoatz, *The Dragon and the Hydra: A Historical Study of Organizational Methods*, https://theanarchistlibrary.org/library/russell-maroon-shoats-the-dragon-and-the-hydra.

334 Craig Marine, "Exit the Dragon: It's Been 30 Years Since George Jackson Died in a Pool of Blood at San Quentin. His Death Still Reverberates in America," *SFGate*, August 19, 2001, https://www.sfgate.com/bayarea/article/EXIT-THE-DRAGON-It-s-been-30-years-since-George-2888071.php.

335 Kyle Shideler, "Black Anarchists Publish Critique of 2020 Uprising and Call for 'Revolutionary Violence," Militant Wire (Substack), February 1, 2022, https://www.militantwire.com/p/black-anarchists-publish-critique.

336 Robert Stilson, "The Organizational Structure of Black Lives Matter," Capital Research Center, June 18, 2020, https://capitalresearch.org/article/the-organizational-structure-of-black-lives-matter/.

337 Gonzalez, *BLM*, 97.

338 Gonzalez, *BLM*, 94-97.

339   Gonzalez, *BLM*, 82.

340   Gonzalez, *BLM*, 76, 84-86.

341   Gonzalez, *BLM*, 86, 89-90.

342   Gonzalez, *BLM*, 88.

343   James M. Allows and Scott W. Jacobs, "Police Arrest Weathermen in Three Cambridge Raids," *Harvard Crimson*, November 18, 1969, https://www.thecrimson.com/article/1969/11/18/police-arrest-weathermen-in-three-cambridge/.

344   Eric Mann, "Lost Radicals," *Boston Review*, January 15, 2014, https://www.bostonreview.net/articles/eric-mann-michael-dawson-radical-black-left-history/.

345   Liberation Road, "Our History," https://freedomroad.org/about-us/our-history/.

346   Mann, "Lost Radicals."

347   The inaugural issue of *The Black Nation* can be found at https://www.marxists.org/history/erol/periodicals/black-nation/black-nation-1.pdf.

348   Amiri Baraka, "Cuba Libre (1960)," republished at *Viewpoint Magazine*, November 28, 2016, https://viewpointmag.com/2016/11/28/cuba-libre-1960/.

349   Gonzalez, *BLM*, 89-90.

350   Gonzalez, *BLM*, 91; Mann, "Lost Radicals."

351   Peter Hasson, "Black Lives Matter Co-Founder's New Org Sponsored by Group That Raised China's Communist Flag over Boston City Hall," *Daily Caller*, September 17, 2020, https://dailycaller.com/2020/09/17/black-lives-matter-alicia-garza-chinese-progressive-association-fiscal-sponsor-communist-china/.

352   Valerie Richardson, "Pro-China Advocacy Group Funds Project Headed by Black Lives Matter's Garza," *Washington Times*, September 16, 2020, https://www.washingtontimes.com/news/2020/sep/16/pro-china-advocacy-group-funds-project-headed-blac/.

353   Liberation Road, "Our History;" Organization for Black Struggle, "Our

Vision, Mission, Theory of Change & Program," https://obs-stl.org/obs-mission/.

354   Influence Watch, "Movement for Black Lives," https://www.influencewatch.org/non-profit/movement-for-black-lives/.

355   Kyle Shideler, "Testimony Before the U.S. Senate Judiciary Committee—Subcommittee on the Constitution," in *Unmasking Antifa*, 22.

356   Robert Stilson, "The Venceremos Brigade: Fifty Years of Cuban Solidarity," Capital Research Center, July 18, 2019, https://capitalresearch.org/article/the-venceremos-brigade-fifty-years-of-cuban-solidarity/.

357   U.S. Senate, Committee on the Judiciary, Subcommittee on Security and Terrorism, "The Role of Cuba in International Terrorism and Subversion," February 26, 1982.

358   Black Youth Project 100, "Black Lives Matter Visits Cuba," August 15, 2015, https://web.archive.org/web/20151204141046/http://byp100.org/black-lives-matter-visits-cuba/.

359   Ellie Dorritie and Cheryl LaBash, "Venceremos Brigade: 'From Harlem to Havana, Black Lives Matter!,'" *Workers World*, August 3, 2015, https://www.workers.org/2015/08/21238/.

360   Movement for Black Lives, "The Movement for Black Lives Is in Solidarity with the Cuban People and the Spirit of the Cuban Revolution," https://m4bl.org/statements/cuban-people-and-the-spirit-of-the-cuban-revolution/; Black Lives Matter (@blklivesmatter), "Read our statement on what we're seeing in Cuba… (read: the consequences of years of US embargoes)," Instagram, July 14, 2021, https://www.instagram.com/p/CRU5kYYp-UU/.

361   Influence Watch, "Common Counsel Foundation," https://www.influencewatch.org/non-profit/common-counsel-foundation/.

362   Chinese Progressive Association, "Together We Move Mountains: Celebrating Generations of Change," April 5, 2013, https://web.archive.org/web/20130411234923/https://cpasf.org/content/together-we-move-mountains-celebrating-generations-change.

363   Kirk Semple, "With Spies and Other Operatives, a Nation Looms Over Venezuela's Crisis: Cuba," *New York Times*, January 26, 2019, https://web.archive.org/web/20190127052306/https://www.nytimes.

com/2019/01/26/world/americas/venezuela-cuba-oil.html; Angus Berwick, "Special Report: How Cuba Taught Venezuela to Quash Military Dissent," Reuters, August 22, 2009, https://www.reuters.com/article/us-venezuela-cuba-military-specialreport/special-report-how-cuba-taught-venezuela-to-quash-military-dissent-idUSKCN1VC1BX.

364   Michael Wilner et al., "White House Claims Violence Incited at Floyd Protests Linked to Venezuela's Maduro," *Miami Herald*, June 9, 2020, https://www.miamiherald.com/news/politics-government/article243266536.html.

365   Gary Berntsen, "The Complex and International Fight for America's Future," *American Greatness*, September 12, 2020, https://amgreatness.com/2020/09/12/the-complex-and-international-fight-for-americas-future/.

366   DOJ, "Nicolás Maduro Moros and 14 Current and Former Venezuelan Officials Charged with Narco-Terrorism, Corruption, Drug Trafficking and Other Criminal Charges," press release, March 26, 2020, https://www.justice.gov/opa/pr/nicol-s-maduro-moros-and-14-current-and-former-venezuelan-officials-charged-narco-terrorism.

367   Rafael Valera, "Black Lives Matter Founder an Open Supporter of Socialist Venezuelan Dictator Maduro," June 13, 2020, https://www.breitbart.com/politics/2020/06/13/black-lives-matter-founder-an-open-supporter-of-socialist-venezuelan-dictator-maduro/.

368   Roque Planas, "Black Activists Honor Venezuelan President Nicolás Maduro in Harlem," *Huffington Post*, September 29, 2015, https://www.huffpost.com/entry/black-activists-nicolas-maduro-harlem-_n_560a836fe4b0af3706ddc573.

369   Opal Tometi, "Black Lives Matter Network Denounces U.S. 'Continuing Intervention' in Venezuela," *Venezuela Analysis*, December 26, 2015, https://venezuelanalysis.com/analysis/11789015.

370   Claremont Institute Center for the American Way of Life, "Americans Deserve to Know Who Funded BLM Riots," *Newsweek*, March 14, 2023, https://www.newsweek.com/americans-deserve-know-who-funded-blm-riots-opinion-1787460.

371   Black Lives Matter, "2020 Impact Report," p. 20, https://blacklivesmatter.com/wp-content/uploads/2021/02/blm-2020-impact-report.pdf.

372   Lee Brown and Isabel Vincent, "BLM Recorded $9M Deficit in 2022—but Still Paid Millions to Execs: Tax Docs," *New York Post*, May 24, 2023, https://nypost.com/2023/05/24/blm-recorded-9m-deficit-last-year-tax-docs/.

373   Isabel Vincent, "Only 33% of BLM's $90M in Donations Helped Charitable Foundations," *New York Post*, May 27, 2023, https://nypost.com/2023/05/27/only-33-of-blms-90m-in-donations-helped-charity-foundations/.

374   Isabel Vincent, "Inside BLM Co-Founder Patrisse Khan-Cullors' Million-Dollar Real Estate Buying Binge," *New York Post*, April 10, 2021, https://nypost.com/2021/04/10/inside-blm-co-founder-patrisse-khan-cullors-real-estate-buying-binge/.

375   Vincent, "Only 33% of BLM's $90M in Donations."

376   BLM10Plus, "Tell No Lies," June 10, 2021, https://www.blmchapterstatement.com/no2/.

377   Caroline Downey, "BLM Chapters Sue Organization Head over Alleged $10 Million Theft," *National Review*, September 3, 2022, https://www.nationalreview.com/news/blm-chapters-sue-organization-head-over-alleged-10-million-theft/.

378   Andrew Kerr, "Black Lives Matter Shuts Down Fundraising Days after Liberal States Threatened Legal Action," *Washington Examiner*, February 2, 2022, https://www.washingtonexaminer.com/news/black-lives-matter-shuts-down-fundraising-days-after-liberal-states-threatened-legal-action.

379   Jemima McEvoy, "At Least 13 Cities Are Defunding Their Police Departments," *Forbes*, August 13, 2020, https://www.forbes.com/sites/jemimamcevoy/2020/08/13/at-least-13-cities-are-defunding-their-police-departments/.

380   Zusha Elinson, Dan Frosch, and Joshua Jamerson, "Cities Reverse Defunding the Police Amid Rising Crime," *Wall Street Journal*, May 26, 2021, https://www.wsj.com/articles/cities-reverse-defunding-the-police-amid-rising-crime-11622066307.

381   Black Lives Matter, "Imagining Abolition (Episode 1)," YouTube video, July 16, 2021, https://www.youtube.com/watch?v=Lc-hovtcCjk.

382   Mariame Kaba, "Yes, We Mean Literally Abolish the Police," *New York*

Times, June 6, 2020, https://www.nytimes.com/2020/06/12/opinion/sunday/floyd-abolish-defund-police.html.

383   Gabrielle French, Allie Goodman, and Chloe Carlson, "What Is the Carceral State?," Documenting Criminalization and Confinement, May 2020, https://storymaps.arcgis.com/stories/7ab5f5c3fbca46c38f0b-2496bcaa5ab0.

384   French, Goodman, and Carlson, "What Is the Carceral State?"

385   Joshua Rhett Miller, "BLM Site Removes Page on 'Nuclear Family Structure' amid NFL Vet's Criticism," *New York Post*, September 24, 2020, https://nypost.com/2020/09/24/blm-removes-website-language-blasting-nuclear-family-structure/.

386   "Internal Security and Subversion: Principal State Laws and Cases," Subcommittee to Investigate the Administration of the Internal Security Act and Other Internal Security Laws, of the Committee on the Judiciary, U.S. Senate, 89th Congress, 1st Session, 1965.

387   Pennsylvania v. Nelson, 350 U.S. 497 (1956); Yates v. United States, 354 U.S. 298 (1957).

388   Andrew C. Mccarthy, "Yes, the DOJ Should Charge Violent Anti-American Radicals with Seditious Conspiracy," *National Review*, September 17, 2020, https://www.nationalreview.com/2020/09/yes-the-doj-should-charge-violent-anti-american-radicals-with-seditious-conspiracy/.

389   U.S. Department of Homeland Security, "Acting Secretary Wolf Condemns the Rampant Long-Lasting Violence in Portland," press release, July 16, 2020, https://www.dhs.gov/news/2020/07/16/acting-secretary-wolf-condemns-rampant-long-lasting-violence-portland.

390   Carol D. Leonnig, "Protesters' Breach of Temporary Fences Near White House Complex Prompted Secret Service to Move Trump to Secure Bunker," *Washington Post*, June 3, 2020, https://www.washingtonpost.com/politics/secret-service-moved-trump-to-secure-bunker-friday-after-protesters-breached-temporary-fences-near-white-house-complex/2020/06/03/e4ae77c2-a5b9-11ea-b619-3f9133bbb482_story.html.

391   Katie Benner, "Barr Told Prosecutors to Consider Sedition Charges for Protest Violence," *New York Times*, September 16, 2020, https://

392 Joe Concha, "CNN Ridiculed for 'Fiery but Mostly Peaceful' Caption with Video of Burning Building in Kenosha," *The Hill*, August 27, 2020, https://thehill.com/homenews/media/513902-cnn-ridiculed-for-fiery-but-mostly-peaceful-caption-with-video-of-burning/.

393 Gonzalez, *BLM*, 80.

394 Major Cities Chiefs Association, "Report on the 2020 Protests and Civil Unrest," October 2020, pp. 3-4, https://majorcitieschiefs.com/wp-content/uploads/2021/01/MCCA-Report-on-the-2020-Protest-and-Civil-Unrest.pdf.

395 Major Cities Chiefs Association, "Report on the 2020 Protests and Civil Unrest," 9.

396 Ariel Zilber, "Revealed: Widespread Vandalism and Looting During BLM Protests Will Cost the Insurance $2 Billion After Violence Erupted in 140 Cities in the Wake of George Floyd's Death," *Daily Mail*, September 16, 2020, https://www.dailymail.co.uk/news/article-8740609/Rioting-140-cities-George-Floyds-death-cost-insurance-industry-2-BILLION.html.

397 Lois Beckett, "At Least 25 Americans Were Killed During Protests and Political Unrest in 2020," *The Guardian*, October 31, 2020, https://www.theguardian.com/world/2020/oct/31/americans-killed-protests-political-unrest-acled.

398 Gonzalez, *BLM*, 81.

399 Kyle Shideler, "Why Congress Won't Investigate the 2020 Summer Riots," *American Greatness*, August 5, 2021, https://amgreatness.com/2021/08/05/why-congress-wont-investigate-the-2020-summer-riots/.

400 Shideler, "Why Congress Won't Investigate the 2020 Summer Riots."

401 18 U.S.C. §§ 1992(a)(7) and (b)(1).

402 Kyle Shideler, "Situation Report: Person of Interest in NYC Subway Shooting Expressed Black Identity Extremism in Online Posts," Center for Security Policy, April 15, 2022, https://centerforsecuritypolicy.org/situation-report-person-of-interest-in-nyc-subway-shooting-expressed-black-identity-extremism-in-online-posts/.

403   Tom O'Connor (@ShaolinTom), "UPDATE: Vehicle of interest found in Brooklyn subway shooting, U-Haul van w Arizona plates AL31408 located at King's Highway & West 3rd Street in Bensonhurst," Twitter, April 12, 2022, https://twitter.com/ShaolinTom/status/1513999908201771017.

404   Patrick Poole, "Known Wolf or Lone Wolf? The On-going Counterterrorism Failure," PJ Media, October 24, 2014, https://pjmedia.com/blog/patrick-poole/2014/10/24/lone-wolf-or-known-wolf-the-ongoing-counter-terrorism-failure-n6936.

INDEX

Symbols

2020 George Floyd uprising 78, 105, 110, 114

A

Abolition 6, 114, 115, 154
African Blood Brotherhood for African Liberation and Redemption 49
Algeria 66, 67, 70, 71, 72, 99, 101, 102, 141, 142, 150
Algiers 70, 78, 101, 102
Ali, Muhammad 20, 45
Ali, Noble Drew, See Ali, Timothy Drew 8, 9, 10, 18, 21, 125, 126
Ali, Timothy Drew 5, 8
Alliance for Global Justice (AfGJ) 109
Al Qaeda 18, 44, 96
ambush 2, 4, 16, 40, 41, 84, 88, 90, 91, 92, 94, 95, 124, 145, 147
Amin, Jamil Abdullah 95
Anti-Defamation League (ADL) 8
anti-Semitism 23, 31

B

Balagoon, Kuwasi 98, 104, 150
Baldwin, James 51
Baraka, Amira 108
Batiste, Narseal 18, 129
Bell, Herman 89, 92, 94
BIE 6, 1, 2, 4, 5, 15, 54, 80, 81, 82, 91, 94, 95, 103, 121, 122, 123, 124
black belt 49, 52, 57, 58, 71
Black Dragon Society 20, 21, 122
Black Guerrilla Family (BGF) 69
Black Hebrew Israelites 6
Black Identity Extremism i, iii, 3, 4, 121, 156

Black Liberation Army (BLA) 6, 5, 40, 69, 70, 72, 73, 77, 78, 90, 121, 144
Black Lives Matter (BLM) 6, 5, 78, 103, 105, 106, 109, 121, 150, 151, 152, 153, 154
Black Lives Matter Global Network Foundation (BLMGNF) 106
Black Muslims, See Nation of Islam 24, 25, 34, 35, 36
Black Panther Party for Self Defense (BPPSD) 55
Black Panthers 5, 40, 55, 61, 63, 64, 69, 70, 73, 74, 80, 81, 82, 84, 86, 89, 91, 92, 93, 98, 100, 121, 137, 139, 140, 144
black power 54, 93
Black P. Stone Nation, See El Rukns 16
Black P. Stones, See El Rukns 16
Bottom, Anthony 89, 92
Brown, H. Rap 65, 95
Brown, Michael 1, 88, 96
Burns, Nathaniel 74

C

California, Oakland 34, 35, 55, 57, 60, 61, 65, 68, 69, 74, 82, 85, 109, 137, 138
Cardillo, Phillip 37
Carmichael, Stokely 58, 59, 69, 107, 114, 138, 139
Carter, Ronald 87
Castro, Fidel 53, 56
Chesimard, Joanne, See Shakur, Assata 77
Christianity 21, 22, 23, 24, 45
Clarence 13X 30
Cleaver, Eldridge 57, 61, 64, 65, 67, 69, 70, 78, 84, 93, 99, 140, 141, 143
Cleaver, Kathleen 57, 71, 78, 137, 142
Comintern 47, 48, 49, 50, 52, 58
Communist 47, 48, 49, 51, 52, 53, 54, 55, 56, 57, 59, 61, 70, 75, 78, 90, 91, 107, 108, 109, 110, 115, 136, 139, 140, 141, 146, 151
Communist International, See Comintern 47, 136
Communist Manifesto 78

Communist Party USA (CPUSA) 48
Congressional Black Caucus (CBC) 3
Congress on Racial Equality 58, 108
Constitution, U.S. 61, 83
Cop-Watching 80
counterintelligence 39, 54, 91
Cox, Donald 64, 66, 74, 75, 78, 140
Crow, Jim 52, 53
Cuba 53, 56, 57, 59, 66, 69, 70, 77, 97, 101, 108, 110, 137, 141, 151, 152, 153
Cuban Revolution 53, 152
Cullors, Patrisse 106, 115

D

Davis, Angela 101, 107, 115
Death Angels 37, 45, 132
Department of Justice 47
DuBois, W. E. B. 50

E

El Rukns 17, 18, 43, 128
Ervin Jr., Lorenzo Edward "Kom'boa," See Kom'boa, Lorenzo 101
Essex, Mark 92, 97, 146

F

Fanon, Frantz 55, 64, 69
Fair Play for Cuba Committee 56, 108
Fard, W. D. 5, 21, 25, 30, 31, 37, 45
Farrakhan, Louis 30, 33, 38, 41, 45, 131, 135
FBI 1, 2, 3, 4, 8, 13, 15, 17, 18, 21, 30, 39, 40, 51, 52, 54, 75, 77, 91, 94, 95, 97, 100, 101, 102, 121, 124, 125, 126, 127, 128, 129, 131, 133, 135, 136, 139, 142, 148, 149, 150
Federal Bureau of Investigation, see FBI 1
Final Call 30, 131
Five-Percenters 131

FLN 70, 71, 93
Ford-El, David, See Fard, W.D. 21
Ford, Wallace Dodd, See Fard, W.D. 21
Fort, Jeff 16, 17
Fort-El, Jeff 16, 17
Freedom Road Socialist Organization (FRSO) 108
Freeman, Donald 57
Fruit of Islam 5, 32, 35, 37, 38, 44, 45, 46

G

Garza, Alicia 78, 106, 108
Giuliani, Rudy 42
Gonzalez, Mike 3, 51, 107, 118, 124
Great Migration 6, 121, 125
Green, Noah 44, 135
guerrilla warfare 28, 57, 61, 62, 65, 69, 75
Guevara, Che 53

H

Hamas 44
Hampton-El, Clement 18
Harlem Mosque 37, 41, 134
Hezbollah 44
Hillard, David 66
Ho Chi Minh 62, 75, 90
Hoover, J. Edgar 54
Horowitz, David 68, 137
Huey P. Newton Gun Club 2, 81, 94, 103, 143, 144
Hughes, Langston 50, 51
Hutton, Bobby 65

I

Ionov, Aleksandr Viktorovich 47
Iran 20, 44, 122, 135
Islam 5, 5, 6, 7, 8, 10, 16, 18, 20, 22, 23, 24, 29, 30, 32, 33, 35, 36, 37,

38, 42, 44, 45, 46, 95, 96, 121, 125, 129, 135
Islam, Ahmadiyya 8

J

Jackson, George 69, 91, 101, 105, 150
James, Frank 120
Johnson, Ethel 57
Johnson, Micah 2, 94, 121, 146, 147
Jones, Waverly 40, 89

K

KGB 53
King Jr., Martin Luther 54, 58, 59, 65, 138
KKK, See Ku Klux Klan 29, 40, 54, 56
Kom'boa, Lorenzo 104
Ku Klux Klan 29

L

Laurie, Rocco 87
League of Revolutionary Struggle (LRS) 108
Libya 4, 20, 42, 43, 122, 134
Long, Gavin Eugene 2, 16, 128
Lowndes County Freedom Organization (LCFO) 60

M

Maduro, Nicholas 110
Mann, Eric 107, 110, 151
Maoist 64, 69, 108, 109
Mao, Tse-Tung 56, 61
Marighela, Carlos 6, 75, 91, 142
Marxist 6, 4, 43, 55, 61, 64, 66, 69, 100, 102, 103, 107, 108, 109, 115, 116, 122, 124
Marxist-Leninist, See Marxist 4, 109
McCreary, Blood 87

McKay, Claude 50
Merritt College 55, 57
Meyers, Tywon 87
Missouri, Ferguson 1, 88
Moore, Audley 57
Moore, Dhoruba 74, 79, 91
Moorish-American, See Moorish Science Temple of America (MSTA) 100
Moorish Nation, See Moorish Science Temple of America (MSTA) 2
Moorish Science, See Moorish Science Temple of America (MSTA) 5, 5, 6, 8, 9, 12, 13, 14, 16, 17, 18, 19, 121, 122, 125, 126
Moorish Science Temple of America (MSTA) 5, 5, 9, 12, 13, 14, 18, 19, 125, 126
Moorish Sovereign Citizen, See Moorish Science Temple of America (MSTA) 1, 127
Moors, See Moorish Science Temple of America (MSTA) 6, 10, 11, 12, 13, 15, 16, 19, 21, 100, 126, 127, 128
Movement for Black Lives (M4BL) 106
MSTA 5, 6, 7, 8, 9, 10, 11, 12, 13, 17, 18, 20, 21, 22, 43, 126
Muhammad, Elijah 22, 24, 25, 26, 29, 30, 31, 32, 36, 37, 45, 61, 129, 130
Muhammad Speaks 26, 31
Muhammad, Wallace D. 30
Muhammad, Warith Deen 30
Muhammad, W. Deen 30
Muntaqim, Jalil Abdul, See Bottom, Anthony 89
Mussa 23

N

National Liberation Front (FLN) 70
Nation of Islam (NOI) 5, 5, 6, 7, 16, 20, 32, 33, 37, 38, 42, 45, 120, 125, 129, 135
New Black Panther Party (NBPP) 2, 94, 95, 99, 103
New York City 59, 74, 85, 86, 93, 96, 100, 120, 148
Newton, Huey P. 2, 55, 64, 69, 81, 94, 103, 114, 139, 140, 141, 143,

NFAC 83, 103

O

Odinga, Sekou, See Burns, Nathaniel 74, 79, 98
Organization for Black Struggle 109, 151
Organization of Afro-American Unity (OAAU) 29

P

Piagentini, Joseph 89
Poole, Elijah, See Muhmmad, Elijah 22
Popular Front for the Liberation of Palestine (PFLP) 43
Provisional Government-Republic of New Afrika 81

Q

Qaddafi, Muammar 17, 42

R

Ramparts 61, 82
Rangel, Charlie 39
Republic of New Afrika 58, 81
Revolutionary Abolitionist Movement 103, 104, 150
Revolutionary Action Movement (RAM) 5, 56, 57, 137, 138
Revolutionary People's Communication Network (RCPN) 71
Rise of the Moors 16, 19, 128

S

Seale, Bobby 55, 66, 69, 98, 140
Second Amendment 56, 83
Shakur, Assata 77, 78, 85, 87, 107, 113, 142, 143
Sharpton, Al 31, 42
Shoatz, Russell "Maroon" 104
Smith, Clarence Edward 30
Southern Christian Leadership Conference 58

Southern Poverty Law Center 8, 13
Sovereign Citizens 5, 4, 8, 13, 14, 126, 127
Soviet, See Soviet Union 5, 48, 49, 50, 51, 52, 53, 54, 55, 57, 70, 71, 74, 93, 102, 108, 109, 110
Soviet Union 49, 51
Stalin, Josef 47, 66
Stanford, Maxwell 57, 74, 137
Students for a Democratic Society 57
Students Non-Violent Coordinating Committee (SNCC) 56
subversion 5, 41, 50, 122
Sudan 20, 44

T

Thompson, Zale 2, 95
Tometi, Opal 106, 111, 153
traffic stops 63, 81, 84, 85, 86, 87, 88

V

Venceremos Brigade 110, 152

W

Walcott, Louis Eugene, See Farrakhan, Louis 31
Washington, Albert "Nuh" 89
Washitaw Nation 16, 19, 128
Weather Underground 91, 107, 108
Weems, Donald, See Balagoon, Kuwasi 104
Williams, Robert F. 5, 56, 61, 82, 93, 108, 137
Wray, Christopher 3

X

X, Malcolm 20, 25, 26, 27, 28, 29, 30, 31, 32, 33, 37, 45, 57, 58, 74, 75, 81, 90, 93, 97, 129, 130

Y

Yacub 7, 20, 23, 24

Z

Zebra Murders 36, 132

Made in the USA
Columbia, SC
19 September 2024

42072243R00105